How Hollywood Got Sex and Life All Wrong

James Bruce

Published by James Bruce, 2021.

HOW HOLLYWOOD GOT SEX AND LIFE ALL WRONG

First edition. August 8, 2021.

ISBN: 979-8215403075

Written by James Bruce.

Table of Contents

Dedication Page

I dedicate this book to all my friends old and new. Once a friend always a friend if you knew me

I dedicate this book to my family old and new especially Chasity and Chad

To the ones I love and shared love

To all the women I have known during my life near and far

To those that helped me create this book and

Dedicated to the memory of Clare "My FIRST Wife," Helen "sexy, cute and cuddly," Robin "Love of my life," Vicki "Meant to be together" And Jennifer "fun, fun, fun"

To God and country for making ALL this possible

How Hollywood Got Sex and Life All Wrong
In the beginning....

———

The Bruce family according to the internet lived in France somewhere in the 600 AD era migrating to England and Scotland where they settled about 1000 AD.

The exact location of the place from which the family name is derived is under dispute. The traditional interpretation is that the name is derived from the place-name Brix, in La Manche.

By Samuel Wölfl[1] from Pexels[2]

It is argued, however, that there is no tangible evidence in support of this and that the name is derived from the place name Le Brus, in Calvados.

Spelling variations of this family name include Bruce, Brus, Bruys, Bruse and others.

For many English families, the political and religious disarray that plagued their homeland made the frontiers of the New World an attractive prospect. Thousand migrated, aboard cramped disease-ridden ships. They arrived sick, poor, and hungry, but were welcomed in many cases with far greater opportunity than at home in England. Many of these hardy settlers went on to make important contributions to the emerging nations in which they landed.

Some of the first settlers of this family name or some of its variants were Alexander Bruce who settled in Virginia in 1716; James Bruce settled in South Carolina in 1716; Richard Bruce settled in Virginia in 1650; James Bruce settled in New York City with his wife Janet and ten children in 1775.

1. https://www.pexels.com/@samuel-wolfl-628277

2. https://www.pexels.com/photo/1427547

According to Paul E. Bruce (Dad) our family tree came from the New York area and migrated west to Pittsburg, Pennsylvania. From there some family members moved to Jackson, Michigan and others headed to Ohio.

My Grandparents....

Photos by James Bruce

My grandfather, James M. Bruce was born about 1885 in Athens, Ohio. After graduating from high school, he worked for the Tanian's Grocery where he learned his trade as a butcher. After marrying my grandmother Mary Oliver in 1907 they then moved to Bremen, Ohio near Lancaster.

by Bremen Area Historical Society

In 1907 Bremen, Ohio, was considered "Oil City." Most of the villagers were in some way related to or were oil drillers themselves. Bremen was a boomtown. The Village was growing slowly in 1884, with a population of 200 inhabitants. However, this all changed with the "oil boom," which began around 1907. Small quantities of gas and oil had been produced by local wells before this, but when wells began producing 140 barrels per day and then 250 barrels per day, the race was on! Bremen enjoyed unparalleled prosperity during the next seven or eight years, then settled down to become an agricultural community once again. Outlying areas, including the private sector, also reaped the benefits of the gas and oil industry. After a couple of years in Bremen my grandparents moved to Nelsonville, Ohio where my dad was born in 1921 along with Albert, Garnet, and Robert who died in France during World War II by a sniper and another younger brother who died as a child. To my knowledge I never met my aunt Garnet, and I have a vague memory of Albert visiting on a couple of occasions. My mother told me my dad and my uncle Albert never got along. Grandpa and 2 brothers bought a coal mine and its was called the Bruce Brothers Coal Mine in Nelsonville, Ohio.

Photo by Pinterest

Grandma worked in a bank. My grandfather was diagnosed with tuberculosis which he got from working in the coal mine. My grandfather and grandmother temporarily separated but did not divorce. Grandpa sold everything he had which was seven (7) houses and his part of the coal mine and moved to Colorado Springs, Colorado where they had doctors to treat his tuberculosis for 6 years. While grandpa was away in Colorado, grandpa sent grandma money to live on. While grandma lived in Columbus with Garnett, they experienced one of the worst natural

disasters in Columbus, Ohio known as the 1913 Flood.

Photo by Herald-Dispatch

Grandma and Garnett had to be rescued by boat. Luckily, they lived in a high apartment building. My grandfather was a butcher by trade and took a job in the 1930s for the Kroger Company at a store on the west side of Columbus.

Grandpa took a new position for the Kroger Company in Columbus, Ohio in 1937.

Grandpa on the left.

Photo by James Bruce

Barney Kroger opened his first grocery store in Cincinnati in 1883, and by the following year had opened his second store. By 1902, the Kroger Grocery and Baking Company had been incorporated. By this time, the company had grown to forty stores and sold $1.75 million worth of merchandise each year. In addition, Kroger became the first grocery chain to have its own bakery. Within a brief time, the stores began selling meat as well as the typical produce and other goods that groceries normally sold during this era.

During the nineteenth century, customers would order the food that they wanted, and the grocers then delivered the order to their clients' homes. Kroger also followed this policy and, in 1913, began delivering its groceries with Model T trucks instead of with horse-drawn wagons. The company introduced another innovation in 1916 with the beginnings of self-service shopping. Like today, customers went to the grocery store, chose their own merchandise, and brought it home themselves. The Kroger Grocery and Baking Company soon began to expand outside of Cincinnati; by 1920, the chain had stores in Hamilton, Dayton, and Columbus, Ohio. Today, with nearly 2,800 stores in 35 states under two dozen banners and annual sales of more than $121.1 billion, Kroger today ranks as one of the world's largest retailers. Kroger - Wikipedia[1]

---

1. https://en.wikipedia.org/wiki/Kroger

Grandpa and his young family moved to Columbus' west side until they were again flooded out by the flood of 1937, so they relocated near the Ohio State University. Grandpa also remodeled, built, and sold houses in his spare time. Grandpa and Grandma shortly after that moved to a Velma Avenue property located near the Ohio State Fairgrounds. James died in 1942 of complications from a hernia. He was 57 years old.

Photo by James Bruce

My grandmother, born in 1888 Mary Oliver Bruce was a devoted housewife raising a family during difficult times. My dad and grandma were close though I can barely remember her presence. My dad and mom moved in with my grandmother shortly after their marriage. In the early 1950's my grandmother died after being hit by a truck while crossing Hudson Street in Columbus, Ohio near where we lived going to the store on April 11, 1951, at the age of 62. She was blind in one eye and apparently did not see it coming. I remember it being a sad time for the Bruce household.

My Parents...

My father, Paul Emanual Bruce's first memory growing up in Nelsonville, Ohio was the use of electricity. "My mom turned on all the lights in the house using the new electricity in celebration of such a great day." "Before that day, she would light up those old coal oil lamps which gave off little light." "I remember how happy we were and excited that day, something I will never forget". The year was 1925. Later he deciding to quit school in his junior year so he could help support his mom. As soon as dad became 16 years old, he joined the CCC's. The CCC's was a new government program at the time that helped people after the great depression of the late

1920's and 1930's. The Civilian Conservation Corps eventually provided employment to nearly three million men by the program's end. Men of all races participated in the CCC, but workers were segregated into units based upon their race. At its peak, the CCC employed 500,000 men at one time. Ohio men also found work with the CCC, with approximately fourteen thousand Ohioans employed with the CCC every year that the program existed. Thanks to the CCC's employment opportunities, many Ohioans were able to cope with the Great Depression. The CCC also benefited Ohioans in other ways, including providing them with improved parks, flood, and soil erosion control projects. Perhaps the CCC's most important contribution to Ohio, beyond employing some of the state's residents, was the continued development of the Muskingum Conservancy District. The Civilian Conservation Corps remained in effect until 1942.

By this point in time, the Great Depression had ended, and unemployment had dropped tremendously due to the creation of thousands of jobs associated with World War II.

Dad not only got a job, but he also got to travel and see the western United States which he loved. He served in the CCC's for a couple of years making $1.00 a day and whenever he would get paid, he would send as much to his mom as possible. Dad was a champion boxer while serving time in the CCC's (three C's). When he was a younger man, he wanted so badly to see the western part of the United States that he and his brother stole some tires to go out west but was caught in Indiana. Because of this theft he spent 1 year in jail. It was the worst year of his life. He told me that sending his mom some money during his time he was in the CCC's was something he was immensely proud of along with the award he won at church for memorizing the Ten Commandments when he was much younger. Dad was a Nazarene by faith and lived as a Christian throughout his life, but rarely went to church as an adult. He did not smoke, drink, or swear, loved to look at the stars on a clear night from our porch, but his greatest love was to work. Dad also in his youth experienced his first movie which was a war movie about World War One and it was a "silent movie," where you had to read the script off the screen. His first "talkie" was a Tom Mix western. Another thrill was to go to the Ohio State University and watch Jesse Owens run track. After the

CCC camps, Dad served in the Army as a mechanic during the war. Dad met mom in 1942 and they were married in 1943.

World War II, also called the Second World War a conflict that involved virtually every part of the world during the years 1939–45. The principal belligerents[1] were the Axis powers[2]—Germany[3], Italy[4], and Japan[5]—and the Allies—France[6], Great Britain[7], the United States[8], the Soviet Union[9], and, to a lesser extent, China[10]. The war was in many respects a continuation, after an uneasy 20-year hiatus[11], of the disputes left unsettled by World War I[12]. The 40,000,000–50,000,000 deaths incurred in World War II make it the bloodiest conflict, as well as the largest war, in history.

Lt. Victor Jorgensen / Getty Images

A jubilant American sailor grabs and kisses a white-uniformed nurse while thousands jam Times Square to celebrate the long awaited-victory over Japan.

1. https://www.merriam-webster.com/dictionary/belligerents

2. https://www.britannica.com/topic/Axis-Powers

3. https://www.britannica.com/place/Germany

4. https://www.britannica.com/place/Italy

5. https://www.britannica.com/place/Japan

6. https://www.britannica.com/place/France

7. https://www.britannica.com/place/Great-Britain-island-Europe

8. https://www.britannica.com/place/United-States

9. https://www.britannica.com/place/Soviet-Union

10. https://www.britannica.com/place/China

11. https://www.merriam-webster.com/dictionary/hiatus

12. https://www.britannica.com/event/World-War-I

My   mother,   Rosa   Kate   Artrip   grew   up   in   Honaker,   Virginia.

Image by James Bruce

A member of a large family (12) that farmed mainly tobacco, sugar cane and worked in the coal mines. Her mother died of childbirth and her father died of stomach cancer before she was 12. Her father was Irish, and her mother was Cherokee/German. Her brothers joined the armed services, and she was the primary caregiver for the rest of her family until she met Paul Bruce.

Rosa Kate Artrip was a 12-x great granddaughter of a Cherokee/Powhatan Indian and her cousins included Jim and Jesse McReynolds pictured below

Jim and Jesse as children Jim and Jesse

Photos by James Bruce

of Country Music's Grand Olde Opry and the Bluegrass Hall of Fame members. Another famous cousin was Wayne Newton pictured below.

Jerry and Wayne Wayne Newton

A legendary Las Vegas entertainer, Newton began his singing career as a child and later became the most popular and highest-paid star on the Las Vegas nightclub circuit. Inspired by a visit to the *Grand Ole Opry* in Nashville, Newton's first professional singing engagement came at the age of six, when he was paid $5 for a performance. Wayne Newton - Wikipedia[13]

His family relocated to Phoenix, Arizona a few years later, where he learnt to play several instruments, including guitar and piano. He and his brother, Jerry, became a duo and by his early teens Wayne had landed his own television program on station KOOL in Phoenix. At the age of 16, Wayne and his brother were offered a five-year booking in Las Vegas, the family moved there.

In 1962 they were heard by television star Jackie Gleason. Jackie, who booked them on his program in September. Wayne was clearly emerging as the star of the act, and brother Jerry dropped out in 1963. By this time, he had signed a music publishing contract with Bobby Darin's TM Music and returned to Capitol Records. Darin also oversaw the production of most of Newton's early Capitol recordings. Singing in a Las Vegas-lounge-lizard style, with minor traces of 'safe' rock, Newton's first single to chart was 'Heart (I Hear You Beating) in 1963. 'Danke Schoen', co-written by Bert Kaempfert, which became a Newton trademark that he has performed throughout his entire career. He then proceeded to Chelsea Records, for which he recorded his biggest hit, the number 4 single 'Daddy Don't You Walk So Fast', in 1972. He also charted twice, in 1979 and 1980, on the Aries II label. His total number of chart singles were 17, and 10 albums charted as well, but it became apparent by the 70s that Newton's strength was in his concert performances in Las Vegas.

According to his official website, Wayne Newton was born in 1942 in Norfolk, VA, to a Powhatan Indian/Irish father, and a Cherokee Indian/German mother. To the extent that this is true, he would not be descended from Pocahontas, whose descendants were almost uniformly Anglo, with some Scotch, into the 20th century. Mr. Newton may be a descendant of her father, the great Powhatan, and certainly has more Native American blood than most Pocahontas descendants.

Powhatan was the father of Pocahontas. Powhatan inherited the leadership of eight tribes, which he built into a loose empire controlling Chesapeake Bay and its tributary rivers, bounded on the West by the fall-line– basically tideland Virginia, plus he had some control over Maryland and the Eastern Shore. As the *Mamanatowick,* he

---

13. https://en.wikipedia.org/wiki/Wayne_Newton

ruled over 28 tribes, or maybe 34, depending how you count them. His domain had a hard core and soft edges. Each Powhatan tribe had its own villages, with houses of bark over wooden frames. They planted corn, vegetables, and tobacco; they hunted and fished. Every few years, the local land would be depleted, so they would abandon the old village and rebuild a few miles away.

In 1607, English colonists of the Virginia Company arrived, hoping to make their fortune (as depicted in the movie). Initially, they built a wooden palisade fort, James Fort, which gradually became the English colonial village of James Towne, or Jamestown. Relations in the early days were chaotic. On any given week, the settlers at James Fort could be fighting with one of Powhatan's tribes, while trading peacefully with others. The various tribes fought with each other as well. Powhatan lived long, and allegedly had 100 wives, with one child by each. There was a dozen known children of his; Pocahontas was his favorite.

Alamy Stock Photos

A Portrait of Pocahontas (2) and her with son Thomas Rolfe in second picture

King James had Powhatan coronated Emperor of Virginia. This made Pocahontas a princess, theoretically outranking a lot of the English nobility when she visited England.

Our Family

Paul E Bruce was born in 1921 and Rosa Kate Artrip was born in 1927. They grew up in various parts of the country, but eventually met thru a mutual friend in Columbus, Ohio. Dad was 22 and mom was 16, fell in love, eloped to Kentucky because in Ohio mom was too young to marry. My parents moved in with my grandmother on Velma Avenue in Columbus, Ohio near the Ohio State Fairgrounds where she was residing at the time.

The effects of the Great Depression[1] were somewhat less severe in Columbus, as the city's diversified economy helped it fare marginally better than its Rust Belt neighbors. World War II[2] brought a tremendous number of new jobs to the city, and with it another population surge. This time, most new arrivals were migrants from the "extraordinarily depressed rural areas" of Appalachia[3], who would soon account for more than a third of Columbus' rising population.

James Paul Bruce was born on September 27th, 1946, the first son of Rosa Kate and Paul Emanuel Bruce. Jim was the second of 9 living children, the first was a daughter by the name of Rosalee whom died at the age of 2 from pneumonia.

The other 8 with their given names were Jim (that is me), Ron, and Don a twin who died shortly after birth also of pneumonia, Cliff, Diane, Linda, Randy, and Brenda. For the first year I grew up with my mom, dad, and Rosalee. I am not sure when my sister Rosalee died, but it must have been that winter of 1946. For a short while I was the only kid in the house but not for long; Ron was born in 1947, Cliff in 1949, Diane in 1950, Linda in 1951 Randy in 1952 and Brenda in 1953.

Dad being discharged from the Army like many young men decided to settle down and get a job and raise a family. After several odd jobs he decided to go to work with the Lennox Furnace Company where he stayed until he found a better job at the Westinghouse Plant in 1953 on the west side of Columbus. He worked in this factory until he retired in 1982. While working full time at Westinghouse his first love was carpentry and built his first house on a lot that Grandpa owned on Velma Avenue in Columbus, Ohio in the early 1950's. Later he built a commercial block building on 3 other lots on Velma Avenue which he owned. Dad later sold all four properties including the house and the commercial property.

---

1. http://en.wikipedia.org/wiki/Great_Depression

2. http://en.wikipedia.org/wiki/World_War_II

3. http://en.wikipedia.org/wiki/Appalachia

**Mom and Dad 1944
Mom said she looked so bad
Because she just had baby
Rosalee**

**Dad and Uncle Bill with Bobby
Aunt Agnes boy visiting
Dad in Texas**

Dad's Military Photo

**Early photo of Dad in
The Army**

James in 1947

Mom and I

Photos by James Bruce

The Old Homestead

I remember living in old house (grandma's) until 1951 until we moved across the street to the new house dad built for us. The old house was sold to the government so that they could build a freeway now known as I-71. The new house was exciting, but Dad had bigger plans and started looking for some farmland with a lot of "frontage so he could build on it" later. That is when we moved to Fancher Road in Delaware County, Ohio.

At grandma's house I remember a few exciting things that happened. One night while we were all asleep a robber entered the house apparently knowing that Dad was at work looking for something of value. He found nothing but as he went into my mom's bedroom, he did not expect to see 3 women (Mom, and her sisters Molly and Agnes) all screaming at one time. You see, mom's sisters were visiting from Virginia and spending the night with her all-in-one bed. The screams apparently scared the robber and he left in a huff never to be seen again. The screams woke everybody up and I remember not being able to sleep the rest of the night. On another day as a child, I decided to inspect mom's washing machine and using my fingers almost lost part of my middle finger on my right hand to an old belt driven washing machine. I still have the scar. Yet another time, while playing tag I jumped from a wagon onto broken glass bleach bottle which almost cost me my right foot. I remember going to Children's Hospital and getting it cleaned and sewed up. I stayed in the hospital with a cast all the way up to my hip for several weeks until I could go home and rehabilitate. It was tough learning to walk all over again. I experienced our first TV while staying in the old homestead. The screen was small, but we really liked to especially watch the variety shows being seen in those days like the Jimmy

Durante Show, Jack Benny, Sid Caesar, I Love Lucy,

All Photos by CrazyAboutTV.com

Red Skelton Show, The Phil Silvers Show, The Lone Ranger, and Hopalong Cassidy.

I will especially not forget the time Sid Caesar during a comedy routine put this pumpkin on his head and was not able to remove it. Being a kid, it scared me because I felt sorry for him, and I started to cry. Mom and Dad had to explain that it was a comedy act, and he was fine. He got the pumpkin off, and everybody laughed including me. The year was 1951 and I was 5 years old. Television was a relatively new media, and the picture was black and white. Oh, and I do not want to forget to mention the cartoons. All kids love cartoons, and I was no exception.

Image by CBS Image by NBC Image by ABC

At first, most network shows originated from New York or Chicago. Beginning in 1949, a few shows were produced in Los Angeles. In 1952, the three major networks each opened a new state-of-the-art television production facility in Hollywood and began relocating their operations to the West Coast. In 1949, ABC purchased the old Vitagraph Studios in Los Angeles, where they constructed a new television facility that opened in 1952. In 1949, the CBS variety series *The Ed Wynn Show* was the first network program to originate from

Los Angeles. In 1952, CBS opened a new production facility in Hollywood, known as *Television City*. They introduced their distinctive "eye" logo in 1951. On the radio, NBC introduced their 3-note *NBC chimes* in 1929. In 1954, the chimes were incorporated into their new animated television logo. NBC's Burbank studio opened in 1952, and their special color studio *(Color City)* opened in Hollywood in the mid 50's.

At the time we moved into the new house our household consisted of Mom, Dad, Jim, Ron, Cliff, Diane, and Linda. The movies during this period featured The African Queen with Humphrey Bogart and High Noon starring Gary Cooper.

The New House

S hortly after we moved into the new house, I decided to visit a Baptist Church on Maynard Avenue less than a few blocks away. I was only 7 years old at the time and I went to church by myself. I remember the good feeling it gave me, and I was really impressed with the lit candles for some reason. I gave me a blessed feeling and I liked it. School started in 1951-52 and I attended the Glenmont Avenue Elementary School for one year.

Jim's 1st Grade Photo 1951

My second grade was at the new Hamilton Avenue Elementary School closer to where we lived, and I remember walking to school every day. One morning on my way to school I decided to take a short cut and go through a vacant field just west of the school when I found a book of matches. Like most youngsters I was impressed with the lighting ability of the match and proceeded to light all the matches and then throwing them up in the air. Well one of them stayed lit and landed in the dry grass and proceeded to catch the weeds on fire. I tried to put out the fire, but to no avail. I ran to school and pretended not to know of the problem. Once I got inside the school shortly thereafter, we all heard the fire engines roaring to put out the fire. I remember them taking a while and it was the talk of the school. I was glad everything came out ok. That field is now where the Crew Soccer Stadium is located.

Dad built this three (3) Bedroom 1 bath residential home plus a two story commercial building. I took him 7 years to build the new house. He sold the block building before he finished it.

Photo by James Bruce

The last summer while still in Columbus, Ohio I experienced my first kiss by my very first girlfriend Marsha Caldwell who lived a couple of streets away. One day I went over to her house to play, and she suggested we play spin the bottle. We would take turns spinning the bottle and if the neck of the bottle pointed to either of us that person would suggest an action or idea as in tag, say something nice or some other action that both parties would like to do. We played shy for a while and tag a couple of times when she suggested that I kiss her. I really got this flushed face feeling and said NO, but really wanting to. She got mad. I got to spin it again and it landed on her side, and she said she wanted to kiss me, and I said very slowly well OK. She did the dirty deed and hey I liked that too. Why have I not been doing this more often. A GREAT feeling and I was in LOVE!!!

I had one more visit it Children's Hospital when all three of us boys had our tonsils removed at the same time. That was not fun, but I liked eating ice cream as much as we wanted. One day during the summer my brother Ron found $5 and decided to go to the store not far from our house and bought nothing but candy and in those days, you could buy a lot of candy for $5, like a large grocery bag full. One day while visiting the store the owner mentioned to me that my brother had been in the store and purchase $5 worth of candy which he thought was kind of suspicious. I told him I would check it out and met with Ron about the candy. Ron confessed and told me what he did with the candy and where he found the money. I remember he was somewhat relieved by the confession and escorted me to the bag of candy which he hid in a hollow of a tree located a block away from our house. A few days later mom told me that Dad was missing $5 and if I find it to let Dad know. I remember telling Ron that he was wrong and should confess to dad, while we were eating the candy!!!

It was also during this summer that I helped a buddy of mine deliver the Citizen Journal, a morning paper for the Columbus Dispatch. I remember when I went back to school later that year the teacher asked us to write a paper about what we did during the summer. I made up a story about printing, distribution, and circulating the paper as if I knew what I was doing, and it worked. I got an A!!! Looking back, it is hard to believe that 40 years later I would be hired by the same company.

My first visit to the dentist's office was while we lived on Velma Avenue. I had this tooth that was giving me a lot of trouble, so mom made me an appointment. Like most kids I was scared and had no idea what was going to happen other than some bad experiences other kids had told me about. All the way there I am sure I was begging mom to turn around, but she said I had to get this tooth taken care of or would give me even more problems. We waited in the office until the nurse called my name and mom took me into the see the dentist where he inspected my tooth and told me that it had to be removed!!! No way!!! I started to get up, but mom and the dentist told me to sit still. I started crying and carrying on like a baby hoping they would let me go, but it was no use. The dentist got the syringe and needle out and I started kicking and crying even louder, so the dentist got a couple of other dentists and nurses to hold me down while he gave me this shot. I really made it tough on them and they had a tough time holding me down. They kept saying that I was strong. After the shot I was totally embarrassed by my actions, because after that it was easy and really, I had nothing to fear. The shot was not that bad. I apologized to mom, and everybody in the office but they were glad I was going home.

Learning to ride a bike came naturally to me. I taught myself using a friend's bicycle because at that time we did not have any. I think that was one of the great feelings in my life and it sure beat walking. The feeling on my face as the wind blew through my hair and the newfound freedom of traveling to further neighborhoods was an exciting time. I took the liberty to hop on my friends' bike and explore the local parks which included Ohio State University and even downtown Columbus on occasion all before the age of 10. Even then I loved to travel and explore new things and places.

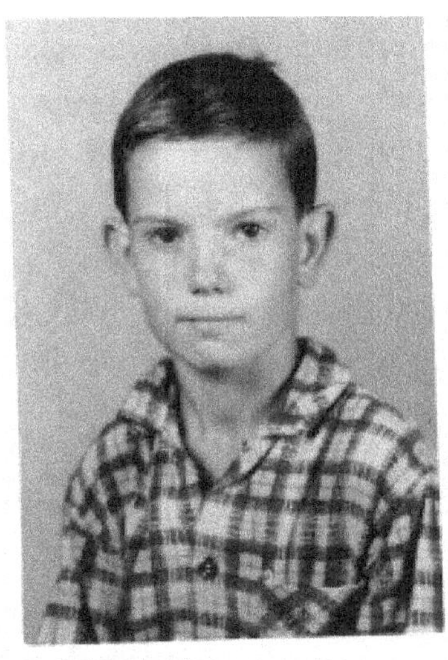

Jim's school picture 1956

Photos by James Bruce

A buddy of mine played baseball and I did not have a glove, so he gave me one but the only problem, it was a left-handed glove for a right-hand player, and I was left-handed. I played with it anyway adjusting my catch and pitch by taking the glove off my left hand quickly and switching the ball into my left hand to throw it. I got good at it so decided to join a baseball team and played Center Field. During that baseball season we took a ride to a Glen Echo Park an excellent location where we could play for hours. Glen Echo Park had the usual playground stuff with lots of bike trails. Glen Echo Park is a ravine park in Clintonville, Ohio were steep wooded banks drop to a meandering creek and a walkway that runs through the park along the creek. My buddy and I choose this trail on one of the steep canyons that came down to the road with a narrow landing area. Traveling a high rate of speed, I was supposed to turn on the road but missed my turn and drove right into a creek bed with a vertical drop of about 5 feet landing on uneven bed rock. It knocked me out according to my buddies and I hurt my wrist including some scrapes and bruises. I was in pain for a few days. This incident also stopped my baseball career. The bike was a mess. I had borrowed it from a friend of mine without her permission. My buddies took it back to her house and laid it in her yard. Sledding in Glen Echo Park was great fun during the winter, I remember going to the theater near the park to watch Tarzan, Dean Martin, and Jerry Lewis and as many John Wayne westerns that I could. I also started to play basketball at school during recess and it was then that I realized I was a good shot.

I will never forget the first time I tried to smoke a cigar. I was at a buddy's house with his brother that lived in a 2-story house where you could walk out his bedroom window to the porch roof making us 12-15 feet above the ground. I thought this is really cool!! We were really enjoying our lofty perch when my buddy brought some cigars with him, I knew what they were because I had seen them on TV. He said "lets smoke one" we all wanted to try one so we each lit one up. Not long after we started smoking, I started to get dizzy and being on top of a roof was a bad place to be. I immediately got down off the porch roof and threw away that cigar!! I knew that I would never smoke again and except for attempting to smoke a pipe during my time in the military I never did.

My cousin Bobby (Aunt Agnes' boy) died in 1956 at the age of 16. We heard he dove into a pond and struck his head on a rock. I remember mom got up in the middle of the night crying. I went to see what was wrong and mom told me about what happened to Bobby. It really upset me because I did not understand death and I started to cry also. Mom hugged me and did her best to explain it to me. I felt better and I think mom did too. We just needed to talk to somebody, and dad was at work. We went to his funeral in Virginia, but mom would not let me in the church, and she told me to go play. The kids all went up on this hill above the church to play while the funeral service was going on. I remember looking down on the church and listening to the organ playing and the people crying. Not only was Bobby my cousin he also was a good friend. I felt so bad for him and also the people in the church.

The year was 1955 when music started to make an impression on me. I loved some of the current pop music by Nat King Cole, Frank Sinatra, Bing Crosby, Perry Como, Doris Day, Tony Bennett, Dean Martin, Johnny Mathis, and Louis Armstrong especially the songs in the movies and on TV. My favorites were the westerns, but the new rock and roll was what it was all about. The first song that I owned was The Ballad of Davy Crockett by Fess Parker.

I heard it first on the Walt Disney series Davy Crockett. The music by Elvis Presley, Fats Domino, Little Richard, The Platters, Bill Haley, Paul Anka, Buddy Holly, Chuck Berry, Pat Boone, and Sam Cooke were my favorites because the pop music just was not as young or as exciting. On the television in those days my favorites included Milton Berle Show, Bob Hope, Jackie Gleason, Life of Riley, Our Miss Brooks,

Disneyland, Martha Raye Show, George Gobel, This is Your Life, I Got a Secret, $64,000 Question, and The Ed

Sullivan Show.

We lived in the new house until 1956 when Dad sold it and it was then that we moved to the farm on Fancher Road in Delaware County. I was 10 years old. Our family was complete Randy and Brenda was born while we lived in Columbus.

The Farm House

In 1956 we moved to a small farm of 16 acres on Fancher Road in Delaware County not far from Hoover Reservoir. Let us just say we outgrew the original home. Mom and Dad made a great couple, but like most marriages they had their problems. Mom smoked cigarettes and Dad and she got into it several times throughout their marriage because of it. I do not remember but a few disagreements other than that. I guess they were too busy if you know what I mean. When we moved to the farm on Fancher we started out as farmers I think it was because of mom's desire and experience from her farm days in Virginia and Dad's desire to raise his kids in a great environment, with lots of fresh air, and clean simple living.

Our farm included pigs, cows, horses, ducks, chickens, and geese. I remember we had dogs for pets, and we also worked in the fields planting and harvesting corn, wheat, and soybeans. We baled hay and straw for the farm animals. Living on the farm was a great life for kids. I loved it. In 1961 Dad decided that farming was not as profitable as he had hoped. He decided to raise and train horses instead. I remember Dad selling all of animals except the horses. Mom and Dad started adding a few horses to the farm these included 2 Thoroughbreds, 2 Shetland ponies, 1 Quarter horse, 1 Tennessee walker, 1 Morgan, and 1 Palomino pony. I think they had us kids in mind which was great. In 1963 Dad decided to sub-divide the land and with the help of my brothers and I we started building houses. We built 3 new homes and demolished and rebuilt a new home on the old farmhouse site. Dad also loved to tinker with anything mechanical. He did all his own mechanical work on tractors, cars and anything that needed worked on. Mom was busy raising us kids and trying to keep us out of trouble. I lived there until I joined the United States Air Force in 1965.

One of 2 thoroughbred
Mares on the farm

Mom and Dad 1965
In front of first home built in 1963

Building 2nd new house on farm

Tennessee Walker called Major
We rode all the time with no gait
Threw me one day when he got mad

The colt Rosa's Birdthday on the
Farm.   This is the colt that broke
All my upper front teeth

Building 3rd new house on farm
With Dad, Mom, Linda and Brenda

Photos by James Bruce

School in the Country

Http://www.bigwalnuthistory.org/Local_History/schools/HarlemTwp/Harlem%20School-1923-1977.jpg

I was 10 years old in the fifth grade when I attended Harlem Elementary School in Center Village, Ohio. This school was an old school that housed grades 1 thru 8. The high school, Big Walnut High was in Sunbury, Ohio being 12 miles away for grades 9 thru 12. I was always an average student, and nothing seemed to tax my brain until my 7th grade when I decided that girls, gymnastics, and sports took priority over school grades. My teachers were concerned. They suggested that I either attend summer school or be held back in the 7th grade. I lacked 1 credit in English and 1 credit in science. It was odd doing 7th grade over again. Everything came easier but I felt better about my grades. It instilled a pride that I had not experienced. I am glad now as I look back that I was held back. However, for years I could not get over the fact that I was to be in school for another year!! All my classmates moved forward to the 8th grade, and I was embarrassed.

In the 5th grade I won a weightlifting contest and a spelling bee. I joined the boy scouts and really enjoyed the scouting experience especially the campouts over the weekend. On one weekend the scout master took our troop to Mt Pleasant Campground near Mansfield, Ohio to spend the night. It was a fun time setting up camp, cooking, canoeing, swimming, and just enjoying the outdoors. I will never forget that grown up feeling I had especially when I decided after the camp-out. I was a MAN capable of living on my own and no longer needing my mom and dad!! Upon my return home I decided that I was a grownup and paid little attention to what my parents were telling me. It was obvious to my dad that I needed a little adjustment. He hit me with his belt for misbehaving and I immediately came back to reality. Looking back, I needed that.

It was in the summer of that year that I fell in love with a beautiful blonde by the name of Bonnie Pullins. I was 10 and she was 7. She lived a couple of miles from me, and it just happened that her brother Dave was in my class at school. I was smitten by Bonnie, but I do not think Bonnie knew I existed or cared. She was too young for thoughts like mine besides, I was a MAN. I apparently had this thing about tanned long hair blondes and a pretty face. Call it a crush or puppy love, but I had a problem letting her know how I felt. That came later. I thought she was the neatest thing. The rest of her family was cool too. Her Dad's name was George, who was a railroad engineer and liked to work in his garden and around the house. He was quite a storyteller and I liked listening to him, so I followed him around when I could. George's wife was named Ruth. Ruth was a wonderful woman, housewife and mother who also could tell a story or two. I would sit in her kitchen and listen to her stories whenever I could. Their children's names were George Jr., Dave, my best friend Jerry, Bonnie the love of my life, or so I thought and Patty her little sister.

One of my sixth-grade teachers was a man by the name of Myron Kuntz who taught English and gym. One day during gym he decided to have a tryout for gymnastics, and he picked about 8-10 kids he thought had an aptitude and physical ability for gymnastics. His goal was to work with these kids and then showcase their talents at any opportunity. I was one of the kids picked and along with a girl by the name of Sally Sheets. We were named co-captains. I must admit I was good but without our coach we would have not known or experienced the thrill of traveling to different events to put on a gymnastic show. We performed at half-time at basketball games and other gymnastic events. We also performed on school stages including our own. I remember being the star and enjoying that short-lived fame. Mr. Kuntz also taught us how to swim at the Columbus YMCA. One night while showing off, I decided to do a double summersault off the diving board. I over did it and hurt my neck causing me to temporary lose consciousness. I had sunk to the bottom of the pool only to be rescued by Mr. Kuntz. Mr. Kuntz was a teacher I will never forget. He taught me a lot about helping other people.

A 7th grade teacher approached a buddy of mine by the name of Darrel Riggs and suggested that we help produce a school play together. We decided to do The Christmas Story since Christmas was right around the corner. I would play the part of Tim the orphan, and as I recall, the play went over great except my one line at the very end of the story "May God bless us all" which came out barely audible. Sorry. During the 7th grade I also experienced for the first-time sports, girls, and music. I liked the 7th grade!!!

I went out for the Jr. High Basketball team because I loved to play basketball in our barn. Everybody told me that I was exceptionally good. It was then that I realized that I was the smallest kid on the team. I stood 5' tall and weighing 100 pounds. Although I was small, I loved to play defense and was also a good offensive player. As a 7th grader I got to play in several games. One game I remember the coach telling me to go out there and make sure this kid on the opposing team did not score again. He was killing us in the first half. I took his advice and did just that! We won the game!! What a good feeling. The first points I scored was on a three-point play after I stole the ball from Kenny Feasel from Galena. I scored a lay-up and was fouled enabling me to shoot a free throw which finished the 3 points. Later in life I heard Kenny became a teacher.

As an 8th grader I had my first date. I asked Nancy Thompson to the dance, and she accepted. Bonnie was too young. My Dad decided he would drive me to her house. You see I was too young to drive. I went in by myself, nervous as heck to meet her parents and pin this flower that I had bought on her dress. Everybody said we looked cute and took pictures. Then I had to pin this flower on her dress while everybody else was taking pictures. You might say I had a case of the nerves. My nerves got the best of me, and I did not want to stick her and ruin our first date, so I let her mother do it. I did attempt to pin the flower on her dress once, but her mom said I was doing it wrong, and she was afraid that I would stick her daughter. Nancy was very pretty, and she had on a lovely dress. I remember we all laughed, and I just could not wait till we left for the dance. Dad dropped us off at the school. Did I tell you I hate dancing? Like most of the kids we just sat there and listened to the music. At a time when rock n roll was big, I did not like to dance but I would stand around, listen to the music and dance to an occasional slow song if asked. It was during this 8th grade dance where a King and Queen were voted on and danced one song together. I was voted the King and Barbara Bolt was voted the Queen. I remember secretly having a crush on Barbara and although I had a date that night it was the highlight of the evening. I do not remember the song, but it was a slow one. Later that night, I decided after a few slow dances with Nancy, a fast song was played, and Nancy and I decided to try it. You see she could dance!!! I am sure she was attempting to teach me to dance during this song. While I was spinning her, my cuff links got caught up in her long brown hair and tore a clump of hair from her head. She screamed, cried, and ran off to the restroom with a bunch of girls. At that time, I did not know for sure what happened, but then I looked down at the sleeve of my jacket when I saw this clump of hair hanging from my cuff links! Yuk!!

I signed up for choir, but it was decided I could not sing. The choir director put me next to the prettiest girl in the choir to help me, but she told the choir director that I could not sing but that I was really very cute. I signed up for band. I first tried the saxophone, then the french horn. I realized that I was not meant to be a musician. I had no idea that I would be in the music business years later.

That summer I found myself, now age 14 still wishing Bonnie, now age 11 would pay attention to my advances however slight they might be and guess what? Bonnie and I started writing notes back and forth. I do not know how it started, but one day after I had written a note to Bonnie confessing my love her mom found my note which of course she read. Deciding to "nip this in the bud" NOW!! She told the whole family about the note. She decided the next time I came over she and I were going to have a TALK!! One evening I decided to go over to see Jerry and his mom met me at the door which she never had done before. She asked that I come in which just happened to be at dinner time and the entire family was seated at the kitchen table. Everybody stopped eating and looked at me as if I were going to be the next thing in the oven. Ruth, Bonnie's mom started by shaking the note and asked me if I knew what this was, and of course I said no. Thankfully, she did not read it. Whew!!! She told me in front of the entire family that I was too young, and she knew her daughter was much too young for such things suggested in this note!! As she kept shaking it, she made me to promise to never do this again and to stay away from her daughter and for that matter stay away from their house for the time being. I agreed and left immediately with my tail tucked between my legs and my little heart broken. Two weeks later though, I was back hanging out with Dave and Jerry.

I had two memorable incidents while riding, or trying to ride, 2 of our horses. One was a Tennessee Walker which I liked to ride by the name of Major. He liked to strut his stuff as most Tennessee Walkers do, but I preferred the normal trot or run mostly run when I would ride him. It was sort of a shame because after a while Major would not do the Tennessee Walk. He was a beautiful horse and great with us kids. If we would fall off, he would come to a complete stop. He would rear up or walk backward and even lay down for us on command. One day I decided to ride Major over to Barbara Bolts house which was approximately 5 miles away to show off a little bit of my riding skills. When I got back home the rest of the kids wanted to ride so I let them. It was too much for the horse and when I got back on to run him around the pasture one last time, the saddle riblets had worn through the blanket and pinched the horse causing him to buck and rear throwing me to the ground. Because of my tumbling skills I was dazed but ok, but the horse continued to buck until the saddle broke. After that, Major apparently decided he had enough of us kids and would not let us mount him.

We also had a thoroughbred colt that we were training to ride. He had never had a human on his back, so Dad decided it was time. After weeks of training the colt with weights on its back Dad suggested that I try it. I hopped on the colt's bareback and at first everything went well, but as soon as Dad loosened the rein a little bit, she bucked me forward, causing me to fall forward. When she came back up my forward motion caused me to hit the colts neck bone, face first, knocking in all my upper front teeth, bent inward. My mouth was numb, but blood was gushing so Dad yelled to mom to get me a wet rag to stop the bleeding. It worked, but my teeth were a mess. Dad took me to see old Doc Fisher and the old Doc fixed me right up by pulling the teeth to their normal position. He suggested that they might work for a couple of years if I take care of them. The first one fell out when I was 42 the second one when I was 44 and the last two, I had removed at the age of 60. I now wear a partial.

Television was great and like most young teenagers I watched a lot of it. My favorite shows included American Bandstand, Ozzie, and Harriet, Wagon Train, and Jack Benny.

American Bandstand with Dick Clark

Jack Benny

Wagon Train

Other programs I liked back then included

CrazyAboutTv.com   Lassie

The Rifleman,   The Real McCoys

Dennis the Menace,   and Bonanza.

My favorite music included of course ELVIS, the Diamonds, the Dells, The Four Lads, Ricky Nelson, The Everly Brothers, Jim Reeves, Jerry Lee Lewis, Sam Cooke, Buddy Knox, Tab Hunter, The Four Preps, The Monotones, The Chipmonks, Frankie Avalon, Neil Sedaka, Ritchie Valens, Bobby Freeman, The Silhouettes, Dion, Don Gibson, Duane Eddy, Jackie Wilson, Jan and Dean, Johnny Horton, The Fleetwoods, Brook Benton, The Impalas, The Kingston Trio, Fabian, Bobby Rydell, Roy Orbison, Bobby Vee, Brenda Lee, Ray Charles, Brian Hyland, Floyd Cramer, the Miracles, Chubby Checker and Johnny Burnette. My favorite movies the King and I with Yul Brenner, The Bridge on the River Kwai, and one of the favorites of all time BEN HUR starring Charlton

Heston.   Photo by MGM

High School

Jr. high was fun, but high school was a blast. I went to Big Walnut High School in Sunbury, Ohio. I remember it was a long bus ride and we had to switch buses at the elementary school. I liked high school and carried a 2.6 grade average my freshman year, but what I liked best was the GIRLS.

Photo by James Bruce

I was too small; 5'3 and 120 pounds, for football but I went out for the freshman team anyway. I was a good athlete that was quick, smart and could play anything. Darrel Riggs and I went to the first practice together where they told us to dress and meet outside. They gave us these football uniforms and pads to change into. My pants, jersey, helmet, and pads were enormous. I could have stuck 2 heads in that helmet. Disappointed I left. Later I went out for freshman basketball, and I made the team only to find out that Dad moved to 2nd shift at work. I did not have a ride to school which was 12 miles one way. Disappointed I had to quit the team.

I went bowling for the first time in a small alley located in Johnstown, Ohio and bowled a 129. Later in life I averaged 157 in league play for one year and bowled a high of 244 twice.

Prior to the football season we were told that we had to have a physical which was done by the local doctor for free. This is a thing that young men never forget, and we talked about before the exam especially referring to the part where he examines you for a hernia. Another new experience!!! But in a professional way, of course. I showed up at the appointed time, the nurse greeted me and did the usual weight and height measurements. I was then told to wait for the doctor. Now this was a moment that I had some apprehension. What happens? Well first he checks my heart, lungs, ears, throat, eyes, and then he asked me to drop my trousers and underwear. I said to myself what the heck, he's seen this before and did what he said to do. He was quick and efficient with gloves on put a finger in my upper left scrotum pressing upward and told me to cough. What was that for? I was told later that was to check for a hernia. He said everything was fine and off I went.

One night in the summer of 1962 when I was 15 and Ron was 14 something strange happened to my brother and me. We lived about 2 miles from the Dave and Jerry's house and walked to and from their house many times after school, this one evening just after sunset as my brother Ron and I were approaching the crossroads of Fancher and Miller Paul Roads suddenly a bright light was shining down on us from a noiseless flying object making it appear like daytime. At first, we stopped, then got scared and we ran towards home as fast as our two legs could go. We could not see the object because it was too bright, but we knew it was there and it disappeared as quickly as it came. At our last reunion Ron brought up that night which we rarely talk about. That is a night we will never forget.

My sophomore year was even better yet except for typing which I thought would be an easy course to take. A course I hoped would be beneficial for me later in life. Guess what, it was the only course that I failed in high school. Typing was the only subject that I took that indeed did help me many times later in life. My sophomore year was the hardest academically and my grade point average dropped to 2.0 primarily because of that typing class. I think about it again was because of outside activities and me not taking my schoolwork very seriously. I did not learn how to study until later in life. Girls, Girls, Girls. I liked girls, but I never got serious about any one girl nor any one girl at a time. I flirted with all of them. One girl I liked called me a CAD!!! Can you believe that!!! Someone that is ungentlemanly toward girls. NEVER!!! The freshman girls were the thing. They said I was cute had a cute nose with a great laugh, smile and personality. That will work!!! But I did not have a car!!! My dad started me driving tractors and other farm equipment somewhere around the age of 12 and I was driving our old 1938 Ford Pickup truck to the local dump at the age of 14. We used that truck around the farm a lot and I did a lot of the driving.

Photo by ClassicCars.com

Shortly after my sophomore year started dad took me to take my driver's test, but on the way there another vehicle hit us in the rear causing some damage to our 1952 Dodge Pontiac. I rescheduled my driving test taking both the written and driving portions. This, I am sure, to a young man this is the greatest event in his life. It was up to that point in my life as well. What an exciting time. I passed both tests with flying colors. FREEDOM is a great feeling. Dad was a mechanic and always had an extra car around for me to drive. I took my driver's test in that 1952 Pontiac, but my next car was the neatest and the next and the next and the next forever.

Photo by ClassicCars.com

I started driving to school shortly after that. It was a great feeling of freedom not having to wait for the bus. I was now able to go anywhere. I wanted too as long as I told my mom. I remember driving to school in a small English Ford with a full car of buddies when we did a 360 on an icy bridge on Route 37 just before you go into Sunbury, Ohio. Now, that was exciting, especially since everything came out ok with no injuries.

Photo by ClassicCars.com

That summer we did some things that I'm not exactly proud of. I guess it was because we did not have enough to do or just being mischievous. One night, while camping out at Jerry's house, he suggested that we go visit Bruce Gary in Sunbury. We hopped on his motor scooter and headed to Sunbury about 1:00am in the morning. First, we had to push the bike out to the intersection of Rt. 605 which was about a half mile down the road. Then we started the bike and off we went. When we got to Sunbury, Bruce suggested we go over to the local IGA store and see if we could "rip" off a few pastries from them. Bruce had seen this semi unload bread, pies, and pastries and such once a week and this happened to be the night. We waited until the truck left and we just strolled over to the entrance of the store and picked out whatever we wanted. We hopped back on our bike and took our prize possessions back to our campsite to eat. We ate until our hearts were content and our bellies looked like watermelons!! We thought it was great fun and so exciting especially since we did not get caught. That summer we camped out a lot and now and then we would take off for Sunbury for a little dessert. By now I had my driver's license so we would use Jerry's Dad's car without permission. We used the same routine as with the motor scooter when we left. So basically, we stole the car and Jerry would drive even though at that time he did not have his license. We got away with it a couple of times when suddenly, they hired a security guy. We found out later it happened to be Bruce's dad. One night we tried again, and as we approached the store, we noticed a guard inside who was trying to get out to get us.

We took off FAST and jumped into the car as Jerry was driving that night. The guard apparently called the cops because we could hear the sirens. Jerry drove out of Sunbury on a back road that goes past the local swimming pool, but as we made the turn on this gravel road the car slide into the ditch, and we were stuck. By now it was 2:00am and sirens were everywhere, but the cops did not know where we were. We got out of the car, and it was then that we realized that when we slide into the ditch, we broke the muffler. We pushed the car out of the ditch and pushed it down the road so no one would hear us. A car without a muffler makes a very LOUD noise. After we pushed the car for a while to this other back road, we started the car and boy did it make a lot of noise. We thought for sure we were going to get caught. If only we could get down this road for a few miles, we would intersect with St. Rt. 605 and we would be FREE. As we crossed the railroad tracks what was left of the muffler got hung up on the railroad track. It sounded like the sirens were getting closer and it seemed that they were everywhere. We started to get scared but worked hard to unhook the car from the tracks. The muffler was hot, so Jerry found a rag in his trunk, and he reached under the car, lifted the muffler and we pushed the car past the track. We all jumped into the car and took off out of Sunbury, never to return. We fixed the muffler at a gas station in Gahanna and took the car back to Jerry's house, coasting into the driveway with the engine off. We quietly got out of the car and returned to our campsite.

On another campout we were sitting around talking about all the excitement of that other evening when somebody said he thought there was another IGA Store in Johnstown, and we should go over there and check it out as well. So off we went!!! Well, we did it again. We ate the dessert again!!! Summer was almost over, and we were getting tired of this routine, but decided we would try just one more time. When we got to Johnstown, we would scope out the store to make sure no one was around and then we would park down this country road a little way down from the store. What we did not know was the security person apparently lived in the farmhouse right in front of where we parked. We ran up to the store put pies and cakes in one basket and headed back to the car. No sooner had we got to the car when suddenly, I hear this shotgun blast that came from the farmhouse. It scared me so bad that I thought I got hit and started screaming "I'm hit!" "I'm hit!" Jerry and I both drop the goods in the middle of the street and ran for our car doors. We were scared, and Jerry did not waste any time by putting the "pedal to the medal." Tires squealing, car fishtailing and we were out of there!! I immediately grabbed my leg and start patting it down thinking I really got shot, but luckily everything was OK. We did not hear any police sirens and we did not look back. It was then we both decided that we would never do this again. I do not know what made us do it, but I was glad it was over with!! Besides, I was starting to gain weight. LOL!!

My first date in a car was in a 1952 Studebaker. A clean car with a neat dashboard and a great radio. My dates name was Paula Freece. Remembering back, at the time I did not have a lot of money, so we just drove around a lot, visited friends, and enjoyed our time together. No sex, just talk, and listening to music -enjoying life as teenagers. Paula and I went to a dance together, but she seemed to want to spend more time with her girlfriends, so a few buddies and I went to a local pizza joint to play pinball for a while. I guess I am a cad. When I got back a few of the girls we knew told me she was crying in the bathroom. I asked what about and they told me because of me. She missed me and wanted me back. We made up, but it never was the same after that.

Photo by ClassicCars.com

My junior year was even more exciting. I did better in school with a 2.3 grade point average, but I started playing hooky for the first time. I probably would have done better in school especially since I missed 27 days of school that year. I never took my education seriously. I only studied when I had too. I again went out for basketball, but I was the last member of the team to be cut that year. I got the notion that the varsity coach did not like the idea that I quit the freshman team. I went out for varsity track that year and made the team. I was not fast, but I found out in jr. high school that I could run a long distance without tiring. So, when I joined the track team, I tried to do the 440, the 880 and the mile. The mile became my best contribution to the team. I also ran the 880. The first meet was at North High School of the Columbus Track Team. I ran the 880 in a little over 2 minutes and came in a close 3rd. I started the mile with the same speed, but not pacing my laps I over did it and totally collapsed on the last turn. As I approached the last lap turn there was a gate which led to the pole vault area. With bad judgment, I decided to go through that gate and take a seat in the stands, but my coach was waiting for me at the finish line with his stopwatch in his hand. When he did not see me on the track, he was worried but when he saw me in the stands, he got really angry!! Man was he mad!!! He did not talk to me for a week and withdrew my name from the traveling team. I went to several meets after that, but I lost the desire to compete. My final meet was at Brookhaven High School where the State Meet was held. I finished last in my heat. The best thing I think I did in track was to help a little-known distance runner by the name of Bob Kennedy. Bob went on to finish 1st in both the 880 and 1-mile run during his state meet the following year.

The reserve basketball coach for sophomores was Gilbert Lakeman who also coached football and taught history. School back then had a paddling way of disciplining wayward kids and I happened be one of them a few times and guess who did the paddling? Mr. Gilbert Lakeman, who was a short stocky man with a temper and strong right arm!! I met up with his "special made" paddle more than once and deserved it most of the time. One time while in study hall a few of us boys were throwing balls of paper at each other when in walked Coach Lakeman. Coach Lakeman happened to be in-charge of study hall that day. Seeing a ball of paper that landed upside my head and on my table, he yelled, strolled over to me grabbed the paper ball, opened it up and read the insides of the paper ball. It said FUCK YOU. I told him I did not write it. He ordered me and the person who threw it at me to the hallway stopping to get THE PADDLE out of his desk. Yelling the whole time, as he told us to bend over and BAM! BAM! BAM! In a hallway that echoed. Talk about embarrassed!!! Talk about pain. The kid that threw it at me apologized and told me it was not meant for me. I got my butt whipped for nothing!! Sometime during that year while in his class Mr. Lakeman acknowledged me after being cut from the basketball team as being one of the best basketball players he had ever seen in the school. That was nice.

Photo by Bikepics.com

My dad bought my brother Ron and I each a new motorcycle to run around on which was so neat! One day when a buddy by the name of Jon Smith and I decided to play hooky, so we decided to ride over to Westerville. Westerville was a neat place for girls, but on our way, I lost control of my motorcycle and ended up in a ditch with multiple cuts and bruises. The motorcycle hit a concrete culvert and tossed my butt approximately 30 feet all the while hitting a stone driveway and metal reflector. Jon could not believe what he saw but came back to help me. He said he was scared, but knew I needed help. I was unconscious and bleeding, so he flagged down the next car. It was an old lady who was just as scared. Jon grabbed a hold of me and put me in her back seat and took me to the nearest medical center. I woke up an hour later with part of my right ear sewed back together, my left wrist sewed from a deep cut, bruises, torn muscles in my back and lacerations of the face. The torn back muscles were the worst part I was in constant pain for several weeks and was taped together so I could not move my right side, arm, and all. I guess I was the talk of the school. I decided that playing hooky was not a good idea after all.

I met lots of girls that year at the Ohio State Fairgrounds during the Ohio State Fair. A couple of buddies and I decided that would be a great place to pick up girls "so a shopping we will go". Sure enough, we met some girls working in a candy booth that were cute and wanting to meet boys and make some money at the same time. Smart girls!! Why didn't we think of that? From the several girls I met that day, I liked a girl by the name of Penny Finch. On another day, a buddy and I took off on his motorcycle to go see Penny and his girlfriend who also worked at the Ohio State Fair. Paying more attention to our girls we got separated. I went to look for him and could not find him, so I went back to see Penny and the booth she worked in was closed. I wandered around until closing and having no luck in finding my buddy decided to hire a cab with no cash on me at the time. The drive home would be about 25 miles one way plus we had to cross a county line, so the cab just got more expensive as the cabbie told me before he crossed the county line. I explained my problem to him, and he immediately came to a stop!!! He asked me what I was going to do, and I told him I would borrow it from my parents. He hesitantly drove on to my house and I told him to pull in my neighbor's driveway because I did not want mom and dad to know I was home. I decided I would try to borrow some money from my neighbors first. By now it was getting late, I did not think they were up being it was near 11:00pm. They were asleep and I had no other plans but to approach mom and dad with the problem. I crossed the road to my house and went in as if nothing were wrong. The cabbie followed and parked in our driveway. Mom and dad had not seen or heard from me all day or night and they were glad to see me. They were mad at me for not calling them to let them know where I was. They asked me who is that in the driveway. It was now time to admit what I had done, and I asked for $5.00 to pay the cabbie. The cab driver was waiting for his money!! Mom looked at Dad and Dad said that he did not have any money for the cab driver. Dad said I needed to go out and tell the cab driver what he said. Well, I went out to the cab driver and told him what dad had said. He said that if I did not pay him, he would have to call the police and they would take care of me. I went back in the house and told mom and dad what the cabbie said, and they wanted to know what I had been doing and how I got into this mess. I explained it all to them and they let me know that they were upset at me. About that time the cabbie came to the door and asked for me. Dad got up went to his private stash and gave me the money to pay the cabbie. Whew!!! Lesson learned!!!

Penny had given me her telephone number. One day at the encouragement of my buddies I called and said hi. We decided that we would meet again and that I should come over to her house and spend some time together. Penny was going to a Columbus school called Brookhaven. Later Penny invited me to her junior prom. We had a lot of fun, but we decided to go to a local Italian restaurant instead of staying with her class which was fine with me. It was a very romantic night!! That was fine I did not like to dance anyway. We dated off and on until Christmas of that year. One of most embarrassing times in my life was with Penny in her basement. We were kissing and holding each other while watching TV, I got very turned on obviously from the intimate closeness, her beauty, and her smell. This was not the first time. We talked about having sex but decided not to until we got married not necessarily to each other. I excused myself and left for home. Not being a serious guy, I dated several other girls at the same time. There was Candy Nocks; a twin of Connie; who I met in church, Paula another girl I met at the Ohio State Fair and Judy Davis a classmate. All at the same time you cad.

Photo by James Bruce

Senior year is always an exciting time. Previously I had worked baling hay for the King family, a local farmer, mowing yard for Dr's Ristine and Arnold and a local attorney who lived on Hoover Reservoir. My first real job was working for the Blackhawk Golf Course in Galena, Ohio and my responsibility was to keep the greens mowed and the course cleared. I was paid a whopping .96 cents an hour. I rode my motorcycle to work at 3:00am during the summer so that I could start moving the greens before the golfers started play. I loved their chocolate milkshakes and gained 20 pounds over the summer. As a senior I was 5'8" and 157 pounds. My grade point average dropped to 2.1 and my attitude was to just get by. The girls in my life at the time were Candy Nocks and Judy Davis. I thought I would get serious with one of these girls but that never happened. We dated occasionally again not getting serious with either one but saying goodbye to each when I got drafted in the Army in 1965. I wrote to both girls while in Europe, but Candy and Barbara both got married shortly after that. The goodbye to Candy was different. Candy invited me to her house. When I got there her sister Connie said, "I should not be there because her parents were not home, and boys were not allowed to be there." Candy invited me in anyway and told Connie that it would only be for a short while. We sat in the living room talking about what I was going to do since I had joined the Air Force before the Army could sign me. I told her I wanted to be a photographer. While Candy was away Connie came in and sat down next me and told me she loved me too gave me a quick kiss and left. That was a pleasant surprise then Candy came back, we kissed and said goodbye. I never saw her or Connie again. I graduated from high school in May 1965. Connie and Candy got married along with their new husbands at our church together. Judy married my next-door neighbor Richard Nichols while I was in the Germany.

The movies at the time included Psycho, West Side Story, Judgment at Nuremburg, To Kill a Mockingbird, Lilies of the Field, Cat Ballou, Goldfinger and My Fair Lady. When My Fair Lady came to Columbus, I took Penny to the Premier. It was a great date, and we really enjoyed the movie. A few of my buddies got together and we went to see the new action flick with Sean Connery as Goldfinger. Both films I consider on my greatest list.

Music during the day included songs by Jimmy Dean, The Marcells, The Dovells, Patsy Cline, James Darren, Del Shannon, Faron Young, The Tokens, The Coasters, The Marvellettes, Gary US Bonds, Ray Stevens, The Four Seasons, The Letterman, The Orlons, Gene Chandler, Peter Paul and Mary, Shelley Fabares, Gene Pitney, Tommy Roe, Bobby Bare, The Ronettes, The Beach Boys, Bobby Vinton, Skeeter Davis, Paul and Paula, Trini Lopez, Lesley Gore, Mary Wells, Jay and the Americans, Johnny Cash, Johnny Tillotson, The Beatles, The Kinks, The Supremes, The Dave Clark Five, The Animals, Gerry and the Pacemakers, Herman's Hermits, The Rolling Stones, The Shangri Las, Johnny Rivers, Barbara Streisand, Lorne Greene, Chad and Jeremy, Peter and Gordon, The Righteous Brothers, Len Barry, Sonny and Cher, The Lovin Spoonful, Patty Duke, Billy Joe Royal, Petula Clark, The Yardbirds, The Four Tops, Tom Jones, Bob Dylan, and Stevie Wonder. Music as a teenager was without a doubt an extraordinary joy and meant a lot to me in my life.

https://en.wikipedia.org/wiki/John_F._Kennedy

Major events during this period of my life included John F. Kennedy being elected President in November 1960. John Glenn orbited the earth in 1961 and the space program started in earnest. The civil rights movement successfully advocated an equal right for people of color which I thought was about time. I believed in equal rights for ALL people. The Cuban Missile Crisis where the Soviets were setting up missile bases in Cuba, which was a little too close for comfort. President Kennedy ordered a naval blockade almost causing war with Russia. Cooler heads prevailed the USA and Russia backed off. When President Kennedy was assassinated in November 1963 it was without a question one of the most tragic and saddest events in my lifetime. I was in history class and the school decided to telecast the events as they were being reported. I remember the girls in my class crying and I was having a terrible time holding back the tears. I think we were all in shock and it was tough trying to understand, or even believe what was happening was real. I thought President Kennedy was a great President.

On the fun side the Beatles arrived in the US for their first appearance on the Ed Sullivan Show which happened to be the largest audience in the history of Television (74 million) in February 1964. Vietnam began to weigh heavily on everybody's mind as mass movement of troops began in 1965.

My Military Career

I joined the Air Force in December 1965 with a delayed enlistment in March of 1966. David Pullins and I signed up together with promises that we would serve in the military together. I think they called it the buddy plan. I was sent to San Antonio, Texas to Lackland Air Force Base and Dave was sent to Amarilo, Texas to another air base. Before we signed, we tested to see what aptitude we might have for military life. It was a difficult day. I did not want to be there, and the result was not good. I scored low and they suggested that I either be a cook or a policeman. I choose a policeman.

My mother took me to the Columbus Airport and after saying goodbye I took my first ever air flight to San Antonio, Texas. The air flight was without a doubt a new and exciting experience. It was an easy flight, and I was amazed at the view from above. It was daylight as we soared above the clouds and into the outer atmosphere, I sat in my seat and peered at the wonder of flight and the sites it offered me from this lofty position. It was a sight that I would not forget and experience many times after this. It was March and a bit chilly when I left Columbus but when we landed in San Antonio, Texas it was nice and warm. A Master Sergeant met us new airmen at the airport and herded us to a waiting bus to take us to Lackland Air Base so we could start basic training. We arrived at the base at approximately 1:00am. Our first stop at the air base was a chow hall where we were treated to a great meal, our last with our civilian look. We were then dropped off at our barracks so we could get some sleep before a busy 1st day in the military. It was about 2:00am when we finally got to sleep and promptly at 5:00am our sergeant came into our room and using a megaphone abruptly woke us up. I was not used to that and only getting 3 hours of sleep was not what I would call enough. But I learned without delay it is not what I think that mattered. This was another especially important lesson.

Photos by James Bruce

I did as I was told and tried to do my best throughout basic training which lasted for 4 weeks. I adapted well except in my 3rd week I got a little homesick and thought about going AWOL. This was not a good thing I thought about it for a while but decided to continue my training. I think it was all part of growing up. And I did grow up as a man both inside and out. It made me tougher, it taught me respect, to obey commands, goal setting, self-care, and money management. Military life was good for me.

I liked the military, even though it was too controlled of an environment for me, but I was going to do my best. The first day included a physical where I learned that I was now 5' 9" and weighed in at 157 pounds. The training was physical but being athletic it was not hard for me. During one physical training session we had to run an obstacle course over and under all kinds of physically demanding obstacles. We were to jump over a small pond onto this swinging rope to help us cross the pond. I jumped, I caught the rope a little low and proceeded to land right in the middle of the pond!! The technical instructors yelled at me to get out and start over only to land in the pond again!! They called me every low life description they could think of and told me to continue the run. I was totally drenched and every obstacle I tried to do after that became a total failure. But I did not quit!!! The best part of the basic training was the weapons training. We shot with carbine rifles and M-16's. We also had to learn how to break them down, clean and rebuild them with speed and then be able to use them afterwards. I was surprisingly very good at all this. I was an EXPERT shot with all the weapons and I won awards for each weapon.

One night a couple buddies and I decided to sneak out of the barracks and go to the movies across the base. We were not allowed to go to the movies, but we decided to go anyway. All the barracks had a guard standing at the entrance of the barracks and no one was allowed in or out after 9:00pm. That night another buddy stood guard, so we felt it was safe to escape and return. It was more exciting sneaking across the base than the movie, but it was something we wanted to do. As we were traveling by foot anytime a car would approach, we would jump in a ditch or behind something. The movie was over after 9:00pm so luckily, we knew the guard and were able to get back in. WHEW!! I graduated from basic training and transferred to PATS (Personnel Awaiting Training School). All the training and good chow helped me gain 15 pounds of muscle. Upon finishing basic training, I weighed in at 172 pounds. PATS was basically a location on the base where people spent time waiting until we could move into a school of training. In my case it was the Air Police School. We did not train and mostly just goofed off for 4 weeks. We got assignments daily that sent us to do odd jobs around the base. We had the weekends off and Monday thru Friday it was a 9 to 5 job. We were required to keep our rooms and the section of the barracks we lived in clean and orderly. The barracks the Air Police stayed in included Marines and Special Forces like the Green Berets.

We had 2 family type rooms where we could watch TV one each floor. One day the TV in our room broke and I decided that we could "borrow" the TV from the Special Forces room. Not a clever idea!!!

Early one morning my roommates and I, 2 twins from Tennessee and one atheist from Dayton, Ohio sneaked downstairs quietly and quickly removing the TV from its perch and took it to our room. The next morning when we woke up, we all decided to watch TV. We watched the news and then Captain Kangaroo a famous kids show at the time. We also decided to go to work late that day so we could enjoy the TV when suddenly, we heard our commander outside in the hallway announcing himself as he decided that he and the Room Sergeant was inspecting rooms that day. Uh Oh!!! I jumped down off my bunk and pretended to be cleaning along with my room mates. The Commander and the Sergeant announce themselves and came into our room which happed to be a mess. They advised us that they were making an unannounced inspection and up until now were satisfied. They also wanted to know why we were not at work and where in the hell did, we get that TV and why were we watching Captain Kangaroo. I guess we were trying to remember what it was like when we were kids. We made an excuse that we were not to report to work until later (a little lie) and we sort of borrowed the TV from the family room on the 1st floor. He laughed and suggested we put it back before the Special Forces found out about the missing TV. Some of Special Forces were complaining already and that we should take care when putting it back. They said something about if they would find the guys who stole their TV, they would personally take care of them. He also told us that we were going to be assigned to be a cook's assistant for a few days so that we could learn how to peel potatoes!!!

On another occasion, one nice sunny day I thought I would sunbath for a while. I forgot was this was not Ohio but Texas where it got hot fast, and the sun got even hotter. Any fair skinned kid from Ohio who was stupid enough to lay out in the hot Texas sun midday would be like a lobster in 30 minutes and I stayed out there for several hours. I laid down for a short nap and when I got up, I felt bumps all over my face. Looking into a mirror I realized that I had spent too much time in the sun, and I had blisters all over my face. I was a mess. Luckily, my face healed in a few days.

Photos by James Bruce

Although I worked at a golf course while in high school, I never really played the game. A couple of buddies asked me if I played golf and I said I could. Well, not really but they did not know. We went to the Golf course on base for my first round of golf. With no practice I was terrible, but it was a learning experience, and I shot a score of 116. We played a few times after that, and I improved my score to a 94. An embarrassing time was the first time out not knowing how to play I teed up on the tee and then continued teeing up during play. I was thinking how else you could get out of the high grass!! Everybody laughed and said, "sure you know how to play" "dummy you only tee it up when you start each hole." Before I left base, I was able to beat almost all of them.

On one trip to San Antonio, we visited the Alamo which I really enjoyed because of my interest in history.

Photo by James Bruce

I reported to Air Police Training School after my time in PATS in April of 1966. This training school was for 12 weeks of intense physical and mental training. We learned about every element of police work which included Law Enforcement, Riot Control, Security, Investigations, Weapons Training and Physical Fitness. I learned a lot about police work, and it was interesting.

While in school we were given the opportunity of selecting 3 locations in the world where we would like to be stationed. It took some thought, but I choose The Bahamas, Hawaii, and Spain in that order. When I got my orders, I was ordered to Germany for 3 years. I do not know what happened to our choice!!

It was during my training at PATS that I met a friend and buddy by the name of David Wellen. David and I would end up friends the rest of our tour of duty in the Air Force. After our time in the USAF, he stopped by to see me at home and he fell in love with my sister, whom he married. After the last day of police training, we all decided to go to the local base bowling alley to enjoy a few beers and talk about the past 6 months and where we were going to be stationed. I had heard of this beer that was only in the western part of the USA by the name of Coors and I wanted to try it. We got plastered!!! Drunk as skunks we stumbled back to our barracks when we decided that we would take a short cut and cross a security patrol area where they trained the K-9 units. Now this was well after midnight and we did not think they were training, but then again, we did not really care, being under the influence. Halfway across this field spotlights hit us square in the face and we were ordered to halt and raise our hand in the air. Drunk, standing up was hard enough and raising our hands made it even harder. It was then that I realized we were being way too loud, and we were in trouble!! They asked us questions about who we were and when we told them we were in the Air Police Squadron things got a little more relaxed. They told us to put our hands down but stay where we were. They had to check it out. That meant they were calling our commanding officer to check and see if we were really who we said we were. This was the same commanding officer that caught us in the barracks watching TV and when he got to the police station, he was not a happy camper. When he saw who it was, he was ready to leave us there to be never heard from again. He also knew we were leaving Air Police School and he was so glad!!

I got my orders to go home for 42 days on leave and prepare for relocation to a place called Spangdalem, Germany. My trip home was another jet airplane fight to Dallas's Love Field, then to Chicago then to Cincinnati. I got an old prop 2 engine airplane that spit fire from its engine as we were flying along at a lower speed and height of the jets I flew in earlier. It was another new experience that I was will not forget and at once I decided I would not fly in one of these planes again. We landed in Dayton and then in Columbus. Boy, was I glad that was over? A brother picked me up and took me home where I had to adjust to being a civilian again for a brief time. I just took it easy running around to see if any of my old buddies were home and I found out most of them had either moved, married, or went into the service. My brother, Ron went into the Marines and shipped to Viet Nam. It was nice seeing everybody that was still around, but the stay was too long, boring and I was excited about going to Germany.

During my leave home the airplanes went on strike, and I had to take a bus to Charleston, South Carolina. The nearest bus stop was in Delaware, Ohio where I boarded my first ever bus ride. I hated it. The people were noisy the kids were crying, and we made way too many stops. It seemed like it took forever to get to Charleston, and it did, it was over 24 hours. When I got to the air base in Charleston, I spent a day lounging around, dressed in our Air Force blues. I bagged my civilian clothes and headed to the air strip to load up for another airplane flight by civilian jet to Frankfurt, Germany.

Photo by James Bruce

It was a beautiful flight and I remember I had the same feelings I did on my first jet flight. It was beautiful up there actually breathe taking. I had never been in another country and the change was minimal except the language and of course the scenery. Enjoying my unique environment, for a while I forgot I was in the military. Walking down a street I was approached by an Air Force Lieutenant. I did not salute and got severely yelled at by this Lieutenant. I came to attention and saluted him properly realizing I am back in the military and civilian life would have to wait for 3 years. We then jumped into a military bus and headed to Spangdalem Air Base in the Rhine Mountains. The trip was neat. I enjoyed the scenery and was impressed about how clean everything was. We stopped along the way at a restaurant, and I enjoyed a true German beer 5000 miles away from home. Where I was stationed, it was cool and cloudy all year. It rained and snowed a lot, but it never got cold, nor did it get hot. I immediately got to work as a security policeman guarding loaded bunker sites, B102's and D54 jet bombers. We worked 4 days and were off 72 hours. Our job was to guard aircraft and their weaponry at selected sites on the air base. In the meantime, we trained learned our policemen's duties, which included security and law enforcement. We were either working or in training but that was ok because it made the time go faster.

Any time we got our 72 hours break we would take off and tour the countryside of Germany, Luxemburg, and France. One trip, Dave and I decided to go to the city of Cologne (Köln), Germany to get to know the people of Germany and enjoy the sites. One morning while Dave was sleeping in, I decided to take a walk around town. I got on the tramway, and it carried me from one side the Rhine River to the other and back. On one side was a zoo and the other side there was a park all within the sight of the Dom, a huge church in Köln. While there, Dave and I also took a trip down the Rhine River. One early morning after a walk, I returned to my room at the hotel I was staying and upon entering my room two maids were cleaning my room. I saw the bed was still messed and suggested that they continue cleaning and that I was not going back to bed. They both started to giggle and shook their heads and immediately left the room. I guess my suggestions meant something else!!

On another trip a buddy by the name of Bill and I visited the Porta Nigra a fort built by the Romans in Trier. While there we stopped at a bar near the bus stop, we were approached by a German and with broken English saying that he would like to buy us a drink. We did not want to be unfriendly, so we agreed. He was drunk. We drank our beers and as we were leaving the German decided to go along with us which we thought was a little strange. Bill and I decided without delay we were going to ditch the drunk German. Our plan was to walk faster down the sidewalk in front of the shops, but he kept up. We decided to separate and run around the block and meet on the other side. We took off and it worked. The German was too drunk to keep up and starting yelling "Which one do I follow?" We found out later that Americans that wear white socks were considered homosexual and apparently, he was interested. Bill was married and I was looking for a wife. Another stop we made was in Bitburg where we watched a movie which was in German with English subtitles. That was interesting. The first 2 years I worked hard and was promoted to Sergeant (E-4) with minimum time and grade which meant I was promoted from E-2 to E-4 faster than anyone in all the United States Air Force in Europe (USAFE) at that time. One of 8 people all promoted at the same time. There was a big write up in the military paper on base about it.

Porta Negra a fortress built by the Romans.
Took a tour of this ancient and unique

Postcard of Trier as viewed from the hillside

Photos by James Bruce

That basic training look
with buzzed Hair cut
March 1966

Home from Basic Training and Police
Training School, 1966 Just before I
Left for Germany

Jim Bruce ready for Security Patrol
Germany 1967

First flight to Frankfort, Germany on a
Commercial TWA from
Charleston, South Carolina 1966

Photo by James Bruce

The most beautiful church I ever saw in Europe was call the DOM in Koln, Germany near the Rhine River.

Postcard of downtown Kuhn, Germany where I spent many hours shopping. No cars were permitted. The people were very friendly.

Photo by James Bruce

While stationed in Germany I decided to go to college and attend University of Maryland Overseas taking a course in algebra. Dave and I, along with about 10 other Air Policemen, were selected to help close and secure the remaining North Atlantic Treaty Organization (NATO) Air Bases in France since France decided to pull out of NATO. It was a great temporary duty because we got to spend some time in France, travel and see the sites, the girls, the food, and the people. I will never forget going to breakfast for the first time at a restaurant in Toul,

France. I was not able to read the menu, so I just closed my eyes and pointed at whatever it landed on. I got sheep brains!!!! The people at the restaurant liked me and fixed me a better choice of ham and eggs. You see I found a few cartons of American cigarettes at the closed post office on base and sold them cheap to my newfound Frenchmen and women at the local bar/restaurant. In return I got free room and board and discounts on everything. We had 2 air policemen that guarded the base at any one time. Each took turns guarding for 8 hours. It was fun guarding the base and being in France. Several times Dave and I each got in a vehicle or truck and race down the runway for the fun of it. We would practice our weapon firepower at the abandoned firing range. When we had time, we traveled, as always, to points of interests like Pont A Mousson, bombed out parts of Toul from World War II. Nancy, a beautiful city near Toul, is where we toured a working canal. I spent some time just walking around and enjoying the people and the sites. I had a great time in France.

Once we got back in Germany a buddy of mine from North Carolina by the name of Franklin had just got back from Greece. When a base alert was sounded that same morning and before we could talk about his trip, we were posted on the outskirts of the air base. Each of us had an area to secure next to one another but a mile apart. The only thing separating us was two wooded areas with a car path in the middle leading to the top of the hill. I was guarding the one that overlooked one end of the airstrip. While walking my post, I decide to visit my good buddy which I knew was guarding the fuel tanks to the west of my post. Leaving my post, not a good thing, I hiked through the woods to see Franklin. The weapons during the alert were live armed M-16's which we had to carry over our shoulders. With my weapon I hiked to the area I thought Franklin was securing. I spotted Franklin guarding the fuel tanks through the woods and decided to put a scare in him by jumping out behind this tree. It worked!! He just about wet his pants. After he yelled, we settled down, and he gave me some idea what Greece was like. He had been stationed there before and knew it well. He told me he had a wonderful time and was looking forward to going back. I told him it was time for me to get back to my post, so I left. Before I got through the first set of woods, I could see my post and on my post was this police car with its flashing lights on. Uh Oh!!! I decided to sneak back in the woods and head for the road which led to the car path back up to my post. I crossed the car path and snuck back into the other woods closer to my post in hopes to get out of this situation by saying I was taking a crap in the woods. As I was heading for my post still in the woods, I hear someone say HALT!!!

Photo by James Bruce

We stopped in Pont A Mousson to eat and cash in
American money for French money on our way to Toul

Toul France where we stayed while we guarded the
Air base outside of town.

Photo by James Bruce

I immediately stopped in my tracks and looked straight ahead at a soldier aiming a 38 revolver at me. He told me to raise my hands and walk closer through these thick woods towards me. When he realized who I was he lowered his weapon. The soldier was my First Sergeant who had the highest rank in my squadron. He was inspecting the perimeter posts. He said "What the hell are you doing in these woods Sergeant Bruce. I said "Sarge I was taking a shit". I knew I was supposed to ask for relief before I could leave my post. Not only that I also left my portable radio on my post unmanned. I was in trouble again. I was arrested, relieved of duty and taken to our squadron office to be written up. The only thing that saved me from getting busted was I had also received outstanding commendations from the base commander while on duty during this alert as well as having received recommendations of awards from the NATO command. It just would not have looked good that this outstanding airman would be busted after those accolades.

While in Germany I enjoyed for the first time buying a reel-to-reel Akai tape recorder and putting all my music which included 34 Elvis' albums and any other music I could find from the library and other Air Policemen. I then sold all my albums which ended up being a mistake. Some of the music popular at the time included music from Troggs, Paul Revere and the Raiders, The Turtles, Mitch Ryder, The Box Tops, Bobby Lewis, The Association, Donovan, The Cowsills, Aaron Neville, Sam and Dave, The Classics IV, The Monkees, Marvin Gaye, The Fifth Dimension, The Mamas and the Papas, James Brown, The Hollies, Bobby Goldsboro, Wilson Pickett, Nancy Sinatra, Neil Diamond, The Bee Gees, Smokey

Robinson, Young Rascals, Bobby Gentry, Bill Cosby, Glen Campbell, Gary Puckett and the Union Gap, The Doors, Tommy James, Herb Albert, Aretha Franklin, Jose Feliciano, Jeannie C. Riley, Tammy Wynette, Jerry Butler, Three Dog Night, Roy Clark, The Archies, The Who, Lou Rawls, Bobby Sherman, and Creedence Clearwater Revival.

The new movies included Bonnie and Clyde, Funny Girl, You Only Live Twice, Planet of the Apes, Rosemary's Baby, 2001 Space Odyssey and the Wild Bunch.

Television which I did not watch much included Gilligan Island, Gomer Pyle, I Dream of Jeannie, The Twilight Zone, and Batman.

The major events of that time were mainly sad including the assassination of civil rights leader Martin Luther King and the presidential candidate Senator Robert F. Kennedy, both in 1968. I remember thinking what in the HELL is going on. I was glad to hear and see the antiwar movement was greatly helping to end the war in Vietnam. The Woodstock Festival in 1969 was a happening that I wish I could have gone to. I found myself feeling especially proud to be an American when Neil Armstrong walked on the Moon also in 1969. And of course, the "Come Back TV Special" of Elvis Presley.

Photos   by   https://en.wikipedia.org/wiki/Martin_Luther_King_Jr.   https://en.wikipedia.org/wiki/Robert_F._Kennedy

Photo by https://en.wikipedia.org/wiki/Neil_Armstrong

DAVE NEVER WAS PROMOTED during his time in Germany, but I was promoted with minimum time and grade. Dave told me after this little episode that he could not believe that I was always in trouble and still got promoted. I told him all he had to do was get in trouble more and he laughed and said he would end up in jail for sure. It was before the start of my 3rd year in Germany the entire 49th Tactical Fighter Squadron received orders that we were going to be relocated to New Mexico's Holloman Air Force Base near Alamogordo, New Mexico. I was ready for a change and boy was it.

Holloman Air Force Base was one of the largest bases in the United States at the time. It was in the deserts of New Mexico not far from White Sands Missile Range. It was a place where we would get no more than 3 inches of rain a year. In some areas it was sunshine every day and beautiful temperatures. Ninety miles to our south was El Paso, the border of Mexico, sixty miles to our east was a beautiful mountain range with elevations over 12,000 feet. To our west there was another mountain range before you get to Las Cruces. Absolutely gorgeous!!! It was a permanent relocation, but for relocation training we were shipped back to Germany for 3 months in January of 1969 and then back to New Mexico to stay in April 1969 until my discharge in December 1969.

While stationed in New Mexico I decided to attend New Mexico State University at the Alamogordo Extension Center where I took a course in accounting. I went to school on Tuesday and Thursday each week and on my way back to base I stopped and got something to eat at this barbecue fast food place. One of the waitresses was a beautiful young lady by the name of Jody Phillips. After several meetings I decided to ask her out. Being shy I went over to the phone booth not 30 feet away and called her and asked her if she wanted to go out. She said, "That would be great, but she didn't think her parents would let her." I said "Why", and she said, "How old do you think I am?" I said, "maybe 17 or 18" and she laughed and said, "no 15!!!" She asked where I was, and I said close and told her to look at the phone booth she looked, and I waved. We laughed and I was hooked. I continued seeing her after school. She eventually asked her mother and she said that she wanted to meet me. Uh oh. One Tuesday night she invited her mom to the barbecue shop. After meeting me she agreed it would be ok. At the time I owned a motorcycle and anytime we got a chance we would go for a small trip in the mountains, play tennis and generally enjoy ourselves. On one such trip we were halfway down the mountain when a thunderstorm pops-up and we headed to the nearest shelter which happens to be tunnel on the highway to the mountains. We talked, hugged, and kissed and then the rain stopped. Another special trip was to El Paso to watch the Holiday on Ice Show. Things started getting a little too cozy and I decided to bail out of the relationship remembering she was only 15 and I was not ready to settle down. It was also about the time I was shipped back to Germany. Oh, by the way, a girl could get married when she turns 14 in New Mexico at that time.

We flew out of New Mexico in military aircraft toward Germany attempting to jet across the big pond (Atlantic Ocean) when we lost hydraulic power to the landing gear. Since we were not yet halfway across the ocean known as the "point of no return" we were diverted back to the states and the closest point to us was Dover, Delaware where we made an emergency landing. The pilots kept us informed and we made it back to the states safely. The aircraft crew hand cranked the landing gear down and locked in place. It was a long wait while in Dover so the military decided that it would be quicker if we loaded on a Commercial TWA flight to Germany. We were then bused to Philadelphia, Pennsylvania to board our flight to Germany.

Photo Public Domain

The next thing I knew I was in Germany again on temporary duty. It was neat flying back and forth between the two countries and "setting up shop" so to speak. At the time this was a big deal and regarded as TOP SECRET. By this time, I was a Sergeant in Law Enforcement and responsible for the Main Gate Post. While relieving an Air Policeman on the Main Gate I met a 19-year-old French girl whose name was Francis. They called Gigi. One night she needed a ride to another town close by. I arranged and paid a cabbie by the name of Fritz to take her home. She thanked me and said she wanted to see me again. After that night she would get the officer at the gate to call on me and let me know she was there, and she wanted to see me. This happened several times and then we decided to get a drink at a local bar and the next thing I knew we were in bed together at a local hotel. Now that was fast!!! I think we were both were EASY and just wanted to have sex. After that, every chance I would get off work I would get Fritz to take me to her place which happened to be another hotel about 5 miles away and it had an indoor pool. Every week on my 72 hours break we would meet at this motel and do nothing but have sex. On one such break we never left her room the entire time. One time about 2 or 3 in the morning she woke me up and asked me if I wanted to go swimming in the indoor pool. I had to be up by 5:30 so I sheepishly said no, so she took off out the room and shortly returned cold and soaking wet. She jumped in bed next to me and told me she was cold and excited. We both became excited and had sex again. Those were the days!!

On another day she bought 2 canaries and this cage off base and brought it on base to show me. That day we were meeting for lunch, and we stopped at the NCO Café. She set the cage down and told me she named one of the birds after me "Jimmy." In the process of showing me, the bird got loose and started flying all over the club. She was trying to chase it all the while calling its name "Jimmy" "Jimmy" "Jimmy"! Talk about total embarrassment! We caught the bird, and she went home. Another time while I was away on one of our love fests my flight went on a temporary duty to Libya Africa and when I got back to the barracks my flights chambers were empty. So being a gentleman (see I am not a CAD) I asked Gigi up to my room normally shared by 3 other Air Policeman and she spent the night with me. It was great fun but not allowed. I sure I would have got busted if we were caught. Besides everybody in my flight was mad, especially my buddies because I did not go TDY with them. And when they heard that I had a girl in our room they got even madder saying something like only Bruce could get away with that one. Again, I was the talk of the squadron. I knew that I would be leaving Gigi and Germany soon and I was wondering how I was going to say goodbye. I think she was told by someone else about me leaving because she did not call on me there at the last. So, I went looking for her and I found her at OUR motel, but when she answered the door, she would not let me in. The door was open far enough that I could see inside, and this naked guy was lying face down on OUR bed. I got mad and sad at the same time and told her I was sorry. Gigi started crying following me all the way to the cab, begging me to stay and please let her explain. Gigi said, "She was in love with me." I got in the cab and asked Fritz to please leave. I looked back and she was standing in the snow in her robe crying.

At that time, I had spent 3 more months in Germany and the next day I was on C transport flying back to the USA. It was great being back in New Mexico's sun, warm temperatures, the mountains, and my new motorcycle. Upon my return I bought a new Honda 350. Every chance I got Dave and I would take a trip to any place we thought would be interesting. And in New Mexico there was a lot to see. We would get a map out of the state and circle any and everything we wanted to see every mountain range, every historic site, every national monument, or site of interest. After we finished traveling New Mexico we then started expanding into Texas and Arizona. The weather was so nice almost every day we would take off on our motorcycles averaging over 100 miles a day. We especially enjoyed our 72 hours' time off.

Photo by James Bruce

Dave bought a Honda 250, on one of our trips we took off for Carlsbad Caverns. We decided to take the back roads over the mountains and through the desert. After we cleared the mountains, we headed down these washouts where there was no road but used as roads, that is, when they were not washed out during the rains. We headed southeast to Carlsbad, New Mexico. When dry the washouts were made up of a lot of stone, sand, and dirt. It was a great road, but a lot of dust especially after we would speed together down the washouts. Dave decided to take off and stay ahead of me just to see me get thoroughly dusted and covered with this white dust. He thought it was great fun and was laughing his butt off, but he forgot one thing; I had a bigger bike, so the race was on. I took off and got ahead of Dave and made him pay!!! I stopped a few miles down the path and when Dave came up, he looked like a snowman covered with white dust and now it was my time to laugh.

Carlsbad Caverns was one of the greatest sites in America, one which I have since gone back to 2 other times.

Each evening during the summer, Brazilian free-tailed bats emerge from Carlsbad Cavern in search of food. Photo by National Park Service

Pictures by National Park Service

Our next planned trip, we decided to go to Big Bend National Park in Texas. By this time, we both had bought newer and bigger bikes. I bought a Honda 500 and Dave bought a 750 BMW. I guess he did not want to get beat again!!! We decided on this trip to save gas and just use his motorcycle, a bigger and faster bike. It was a great ride through southern New Mexico and into the Big Bend part of Texas. Wow!!! It was great weather as usual, and the National Park was beautiful. The mountain cliffs and the Rio Grande River running through this area made a great contrast and something special. After spending the night in the area, we took off the next day for New Mexico. On our way back about halfway to El Paso the bottom of the gas filter fell out causing us to lose fuel fast and the engine died. We were in the middle of nowhere and basically had little gas left. It was hot and dry, in this part of Texas and we had no food or water. First, we worked on getting the motorcycle fixed looking for the lost parts on the road, which we never found. Next, we thought of ways to rig the filter bottom and come up with some parts in the ditch, and some material in our toolbox. Now we needed some gas. Little traffic came down the road but when we saw a pickup truck heading our way, we flagged the driver down. He gave us some gas and asked me if we needed some water, I said no. I must have been delirious cause we were dying of thirst. Dave came to our rescue and spoke up, so the driver also gave us some water. We thanked him and he wished us well. The strange looking parts worked, and we made it to the nearest gas station on fumes.

Photo by National Park Service

Photo by National Park Service

When I worked as the Dispatcher in the Police Squadron's Office, I got all the orders for every day straight from the commander. One day I was told that the entire base was going on Exercise ALERT but luckily for Dave and me we were getting off our shift before the Alert started. We wasted no time in getting off the base and we decided to take advantage of this extra time and headed for Las Vegas, Nevada. I owned a 1962 Chevy Impala, so we decided to take it this time and leave our bikes at the base. We really did not have a lot of planning time, so we forgot or did not have enough money to get all the way to Las Vegas. Halfway to Las Vegas we determined we had enough money and gas for a trip to the Grand Canyon so off we went. Back then there were not a lot of gas stations in this part of the country. This was something we had not planned on, so we got a little worried when we realized we needed gas to get back to the base. We made it to the Grand Canyon South Rim early that morning about 2:00am. There was no place to spend the night, so we slept in my car. At sunrise I witnessed possibly one of the most beautiful sights one can experience, a sunrise at the South Rim of the Grand Canyon. I have seen pictures of the Grand Canyon before but nothing and I mean nothing prepared me for this. At first, we did not realize that it had snowed and there was a rainbow forming in the sky. What a remarkable sight!! We did not have a lot of time to visit so we started looking for gas for my car. We found it in the park, but the gas was twice as much as usual (.50 cents per gallon). We made it back to the base just as the alert was over. Now that was planning!

Photo by National Park Service

While stationed in New Mexico I also visited Mexico at El Paso. My visit to Mexico was also a new experience. Many people and places in Mexico were poor, as we walked the streets I negotiated and bought a Chess Set made from quartz. I was saddened by the sight of a little girl begging for money just inside the border. I did not have a lot of money, but I gave her what I could. I hope she benefited from the gift. It made me feel good. Another time I picked up a homeless hitch hiker and without saying a word as he was getting out of my car, I gave him some money. He looked hungry. One of our trips was a trip to Colorado to see the Royal Gorge. On the way, we stopped at the Colorado National Monument where we drove the 22-mile Rim Drive so we could catch the beautiful splendor that only God's nature can afford. What a road and what sights we saw. Dave mentioned what a ride this would have been on our motorcycles. The Royal Gorge is a suspension bridge that at the time was considered the highest in the world. We drove across the bridge and took in all the beauty the area had to offer. As we drove across the bridge the wind was strong that day. The bridge was swaying as we drove across it. It was a little scary but worth the ride. Other trips Dave and I included the Sierra Blanca, a 12003 ft. mountain peak in New Mexico, and Fort Courage home of the F Troop (TV show), located in Houck, Arizona. This was where the popular TV series was shot. White Sands National Monument is where I spent several days just enjoying the sun. On one day while visiting the White Sands alone I decided to go for a walk in the nude. The temperature was around 100 degrees and it felt good.

Royal Gorge

Picture by Wikipedia

One evening a few of my buddies decided to visit a dance hall in Las Cruces in hopes of meeting some girls and get lucky. One of my buddies was named Bob Hope a nephew of the Legendary Bob Hope the entertainer. We got plastered and when I get plastered, I can dance or so I thought. I met this girl which started out casually but got hotter by the hour. We danced and she decided to sit with me, and we got closer and closer and then we decided to dance again when by this time I was feeling good. My dancing got sloppy and as I was dancing, I hit this huge guy with my swinging elbows. I did not really mean it, but he did, and he stopped dancing and was sizing me up for a punch. Apparently deciding I was too drunk, he told me to go take a seat. I looked up at him and decided I would!! My girl and I decided to head for my car for some heavy petting when up drives her husband which she forgot to tell me about. I escaped yet another fight and something told me it was time to go home. She went into the club with her husband, and I went to my car to pass out. On the way back to base we had to stop several times to throw up and in one case Bob did not make it out of my car and puked in my beautiful 1962 Chevy. It was time to buy a new car anyway.

I went shopping and bought a brand new 1969 Pontiac GTO. It had the largest engine in it that year of any conventional car. It was gold inside and out. It was built for speed and speed I did just that. A buddy of mine borrowed the GTO and without telling me raced it against a Dodge Roadrunner supposably the two fastest cars on the road that year. My buddy and my Goat won!!! He bragged about it for the rest of my time in service and although I was upset, I was proud too. I had the fastest car on the base.

Photo by Streetside Classics

During a trip home to Ohio on leave I was behind two semi-trucks when I got tired of staying behind them, so I just floored it while going down this big hill in Arkansas. I passed up the two semis standing still, but by the time I got pass them I had to pass them going up the hill. There was a State Patrol at the bottom of the hill. I had to be doing over 90 mph when I crossed back over the line going up the hill. Of course, the State Patrol turned on his lights and I immediately pulled over to receive my tickets. What a way to start out a leave. The officer was polite and complimented me on my car saying I could not have done that with any other car. He did not ticket me for speed but for crossing the line. He escorted me to the police station because I was from out of state. When I got to the police station the officer took me to the clerk to process my ticket. When the commander heard that I was an Air Policeman on leave, he asked me to come into his office. I told him what happened. He listened intently and suggested that I take the ticket with me and mail the money and a copy of the ticket. He knew that I was in the military, and I did not have a lot of money for the fine. He told me that if for some reason I did not send it in as suggested that I not be stopped in Missouri again or I would be fined and thrown in jail. I got the point and thanked him for being so considerate. I never sent in the fine.

It was great being home after being in Germany and now stationed in New Mexico for a while. I had not seen my family for almost 3 years and of course I had to show off my new 1969 GTO. It was during this leave that I had to decide if I wanted to remain in the military or return to civilian life. I decided to wait to make that decision upon my return to New Mexico.

Back at Holliman Air Force Base I was promoted to Non-Commission Officer in Charge (NCOIC) of The Traffic Department. I really liked my new position, and I was responsible for all traffic law enforcement for the entire base. I had a special squadron of law enforcement policemen that directed traffic at key locations throughout the base. I was also responsible for all traffic accident investigations.

photos by

James Bruce

This made it hard for me to decide if I wanted to stay in the Air Force, but because I was overlooked on my rank to E-5, I decided it was time to leave the military. Also, I got into a little trouble during my last week of service.

Now realizing that I was SHORT meaning I was leaving the military soon I partied hard and decided to oversleep on just this one day. Most of the people in my squadron were dependable and needed little supervision, but this new airman by the name of Gable that I had just hired decided to squeal. He told my commanding officer about me not showing up for work that day. A lot of people were getting out on early release because of the downsizing of Vietnam, and I was one of them. The squadron master sergeant had decided that this neglect of duty on my part should be made an example. He wrote me up and relived me of duty and told me to report to my squadron commander, Captain Ross. Captain Ross and I had been together for all my tour of duty. He knew all about my life as an air policeman. In his office that day, we shared some of our military life together with some laughs and some tears. That is what it is all about, plus he was mad because he got passed over for promotion in his last review like I had. He told me they wanted to make me an example, be busted to airman basic and receive a dishonorable discharge, but because of our friendship and my exemplary military career he just could not do it. Instead, he suggested that I work in security on the flight line for the next 3 days my last 3 days of my Air Force Career. I gladly accepted, thanked him, and wished him well. With my rank in tack and my honorable discharge in hand I went back to a different world in civilian life.

Home Sweet Home

It was December 1969, and I was home. A lot had changed in almost 4 years. All my old girl friends and buddies had married, moved, gone to school or in the military. My brother Ron joined the Marines and was serving in Viet Nam his second tour of duty. Cliff had joined the Navy. Randy, Diane, Linda and Brenda were still living at home with mom and dad, who were now in their 40's. Things seemed a lot quieter. I was FREE and out of the service.

It felt good but my life had no direction or desire to get serious about anything. I knew that would change so I started to look for work to help pay for my GTO. My dad got me a job at his Westinghouse Plant which I did not like. I think I worked a total of 4 hours before I decided I had enough of factory line work. I left at lunch never to return. The I went to interview for a job at several Temporary Service locations but had no luck until I finally accepted a starting position a Elston Richards Storage Company as a billings clerk for $2.70 cents per hour.

It was January 1970, after clocking out, I walked out to the parking lot at my new job when I realized my GTO was missing. I figured a hot car like my goat was stolen so I went back inside to call the cops. They made a report and suggested that I call my finance company. My finance company told me they had my car because I was 2 months past due. It was repossessed!!! I called my mom and she told me she would help me get back my car and she would come and pick me up. Thanks Mom. You know moms are great. I liked my job and the people I worked with, and I made it a point to work hard and learn as much as possible. My bosses liked me and again I was promoted whenever possible.

In the meantime, back at home, because I was not making enough money, I was living at home basically free. One day while rummaging through the refrigerator, Dad had had enough of "freeloader" Jim. He told me it was time to leave the nest again!!! Ron had just got out of the Marines and he and his girlfriend had just bought a house from Dad and that I could move into with them temporarily. Moving was easy because they lived only 2 houses down the street. I did not have a lot to move like only my clothes and I did not have a whole lot of those.

One day Mom asked Cliff (brother) and I if we would go pickup our brother Ron at the Marine Base located in North Carolina. Of course, we would! We took off in my GTO. It was a comfortable ride in my goat, and we made it down there I am sure in record time. Somewhere in North Carolina while driving down a two-lane road at dusk I found myself again behind a Semi Tractor Trailer going too slow for me and you guessed it, I decided to pass. I floored the GTO and off we went flying around the Semi. Suddenly over a small hill pops up another car heading right at us. Knowing what the GTO would do I made a split decision to put the pedal to the medal which I am sure putting us almost to 90 miles an hour all the while Cliff was screaming "WE'RE GOING TO DIE". The other car drove safely into the ditch, and we left the semi in the dust.

1970 brought us the music of The Carpenters, Jackson 5, Anne Murray, Chicago, James Taylor, Ike and Tina Turner, Joe Cocker, Stills Nash and Young. At the big screen we saw Five Easy Pieces, Little Big Man, Patton, Love Story, Mash and Airport. On the little screen we were entertained with The Flip Wilson Show, The Six Million Dollar Man, The Incredible Hulk, Bonanza, Rowan and Martin's Laugh In, Hee Haw and My Three Sons. The major events of that year were the National Guard opened fire killing 4 students at Kent State University. I remember this vividly, it made me very mad and asking why. Sad so, so senseless. The Beatles breakup and Janis Joplin died during this year.

Photo by James Bruce

Ron Bruce (My Brother) Marine in Viet Nam 2 Tours / Wounded and Malaria

John Filo[1]'s Pulitzer Prize[2]-winning photograph of Mary Ann Vecchio[3] kneeling over the body of Jeffrey Miller[4] minutes after the unarmed student was fatally shot by an Ohio National Guardsman[5].

1. https://en.wikipedia.org/wiki/John_Filo

2. https://en.wikipedia.org/wiki/Pulitzer_Prize

3. https://en.wikipedia.org/wiki/Mary_Ann_Vecchio

4. https://en.wikipedia.org/wiki/Jeffrey_Miller_(shooting_victim)

5. https://en.wikipedia.org/wiki/Ohio_Army_National_Guard

Clare and I

That summer I met a girl that I had known as a little girl who worked for her dad at the Schott Marina by the name of Clare Eileen Schott. She was 19, and occasionally dated my brother Randy who was only 16. Randy could not take her to the Westerville 4th of July Celebration and mentioned to me she really wanted to go. We went and we really had a wonderful time. I did not know it then, but this was the first date with my future wife. We were inseparable after that first date and as they say, "fell in love and got married." Clare and I were married June 5, 1971. In the last five years I had dreamed many times about meeting the right girl and getting married. I was really looking forward to that part of my life. It was now at this time in my life that I really liked the idea of marriage, settling down and having kids. I was 25.

Clare Eileen Schott Bruce / Photo by James Bruce

During our engagement period I knew we were not meant for each other, but because of this burning desire to settle down and Clare was a bright and beautiful girl, I wanted to give this relationship a try. Part of the engagement process at the St. Paul Lutheran church was to attend new marriage counseling classes. This was the same church that we both had Catechism and was baptized in. The Pastor was great but after the classes he knew we were worlds apart and told us both that he did not think it would work. We did not care. We had each other and that is all that mattered.

St Paul Lutheran Church today/ Photo by James Bruce

Photo by James Bruce

Clare was on the pill, so we took advantage of our new sexual freedom. We were together every single day except one during that time. After the wedding held at the St. Paul Lutheran Church, we grew up in we honeymooned at the beautiful Nags Head Beach on the coast of North Carolina. We left our apartment and ate breakfast at a buffet nearby. Off we went toward the southeast coast. We hit the Blue Ridge Mountains that evening in a rush to get to our destination. Driving like a mad man I came down with the worst upset stomach or food poisoning that a fellow could have. That night I suffered and had to set on the toilet the entire evening with a bucket in front of me. I felt sorry for Clare, but she was very understanding and was scared for me because I was so sick. She was so scared that she cried at times.

Our honeymoon was different just like we were. The pastor warned us. We lived together for almost 6 months before we were married, and we had a good time but after we were married our relationship started to change and our honeymoon was the start of a rocky marriage. I guess I had too high of expectations. We both had tough times not understanding or caring enough maybe because we were immature or different. I wanted to travel and enjoy the sights and she preferred to stay at the hotel and shop. I planned our honeymoon so we could take in the Blue Ridge Parkway making a stop in Jamestown, Virginia where local hero Sgt Alvin C. York was once touted by Gen. John J. Pershing as "the greatest soldier of the war." The war was World War I and the man would win the Medal of Honor. Sergeant York the movie was one of my personal favorites. In the movie Sgt. York was portrayed by Gary Cooper.

The Parkway rambles along the crest of the Blue Ridge Mountains all the way to the Great Smokies. From lofty summits of the Blue Ridge Mountains along the way, a series of spectacular views of the Shenandoah Valley spreads before you. We made a stop in Luray, Virginia to see one of the most beautiful caves in the world. Luray Caverns that boast elaborate colorful rock formations and the only stalactite organ in existence. Our next stop was the Great Smoky Mountains National Park with all its beauty and splendor. This is the most visited national park in the country. The wondrous Smokies get their name from the blue haze that hovers over mossy mountain peaks. We made it a point to climb up the observation tower atop 6,643-foot Clingmans Dome and travel the 11-mile loop drive passing many of the restored structures of this isolated mountain community that was founded in 1819. Although we did not stay long, what we saw was really neat. I must say, my first experience visiting the Blue Ridge Mountains was an awesome experience. From the Smokies we traveled to the Appomattox Courthouse National Historical Park where the Treaty of the Civil War was signed and of course all the sights of the Carolina Coast. The weather was good, and I got out as much as possible. Clare's bikini was stolen off the clothesline the second night there. That made her mad. I bought this Styrofoam Surfboard to try to surf. I did until one day I got into small, but powerful, surf going the wrong way (sideways) and took a spill. It caused me to hit the rough beach bottom hard and broke my surfboard. I guess my surfing career was a short one. Another time I took this air floating device out and while just lying there and enjoying the sun I looked up and our motel was a good bit of distance away more than it should be. Apparently, the surf was up, and it caused me to drift out towards the ocean waters. After a long struggle, paddling I made it back to shore.

Jim resting before the big trip and
After an exciting night with Clare

The road to outer banks of North
Carolina. First ocean experience.

That's Jim heading for the surf with
A new board.

That's me coming back with one half
A board after my accident in the surf

Our ocean front room where we stayed
While on the outer banks.

The floating device almost cost me my
Life. I almost floated to far from shore.

Photos by James Bruce

The Blue Ridge Parkway was a beautiful Drive with wonderful views of the valley below like these.

Another absolutely grand site from the Parkway.

Clare and I hiked this Smokey Mountain walkway to the tower

The tower on the left and the view on the right is atop one of the highest mountain peaks in the Smokey Mountain National Park

Photos by James Bruce

Photos by James Bruce

While I was working at Elston Richards in late 1971 I started a repair business that I was able to run out of the Elston Richards warehouse. I repaired appliances for the Whirlpool Corporation. I hired two friends from high school, Jerry Pullins and Jon Smith as repairmen and we took in their damaged appliances and repaired them. We used new parts so they could re-stock them to their inventory. It was a thriving business that lasted only about 6 months, but I was able to save enough money from this venture to put a down payment on a new house for Clare and myself. It was located on the beautiful Lake Choctaw near London, Ohio. It was a beautiful cape cod style home with 3 bedrooms and 2 baths plus a 2-car attached garage on a large lot and sat on the east side of the lake. The year was 1972 and we paid $34,000 for it.

At first, our marriage was everything I expected it to be but each year after that I realized we were missing something, and I felt it was kids. Clare was on the pill, and we decided that we should wait to have kids when we were better prepared to afford them. Although we could afford them later it was never brought up again. She remained on the pill our entire marriage. Sex was great at first, but after the newness was over, we both seemed to lose interest. We stopped communicating and both of us started to not enjoy our time together. It was almost like we liked being away from each other and enjoying the things we individually liked. After sex we did not have a lot to offer the marriage. This eventually broke down our relationship and we totally were made aware of the marriage was over.

The first couple of years our marriage went well, and we both loved to travel. We made it a point to visit all the beautiful places and locations including the State Parks in Ohio and the surrounding states. During our travels we vacationed in Indiana, Illinois, Kentucky, Missouri, Oklahoma, Texas, New Mexico, Arizona, Utah, Colorado, Kansas, Pennsylvania, New York, West Virginia, Virginia, Maryland, North Carolina, Michigan, Alabama, Mississippi, and Canada.

In 1973 I planned a trip with Clare, my sister Diane and Dave Wellen (my old Air Force buddy) and my youngest sister Brenda and her husband Doug. We visited the Abraham Lincoln Birthplace National Historic Site. A massive granite memorial encases the log cabin where the Great Emancipator was born February 12, 1809, on the original 116-acre Lincoln farm. We also stopped at a wondrous site known as Cumberland Falls State Park and the main feature was the falls dropped 68 feet and 125 feet wide. The highlight of this trip was to visit the nation's longest caverns in Kentucky called the Mammoth Caverns. We choose two different trips to take. One of them was a short walk to the Niagara Falls section and then the other one was an 8-hour tour of the lower level of the cavern. The short trip was easy and unique for caverns with a final look at a formation of stalagmites that created a Niagara Falls like image.

Photos by James Bruce

We camped in tents that night at a camp site nearby. We all fell asleep, fast worn out by the trip there and the walk in the caverns. And sleep sound we did until early the next morning, when Clare and I were awakened by a sound of a mad bull outside our tent. Startled, we rushed out of our tent with just our underwear only to be surprised and laughed at by Dave, Diane, Brenda, and Doug. Dave had the horn in his hand! After a few good laughs, we headed for the Caverns to take an 8-hour tour through the lower level. When we got there, we were outfitted with knee pads and a head lantern being told we would be using them a lot. The first part of the tour was easy and very enjoyable. As we got deeper in the caves, we had to use the lights from our helmet to see and as we got even deeper at times we had to crawl through the cavern. We lunched at the halfway point on a lunch box provided by the park and for a few minutes we were told to turn off our lights on our helmets to experience total darkness. We did, and believe me, it was totally dark down there. We saw sights you can only experience deep underground and some areas of the tour were difficult, but we really enjoyed the tour.

On another trip Clare and I decided to take was a canoe trip down a creek near the Mohican State Park in Ohio. It was a great weather day for canoeing and our plan was to canoe down this creek for about 12 miles and be picked up by a bus and returned to our car. It all started out fine until we got to some rapids on a bend in the creek. Several canoes got stuck because of the current and other canoes were blocking the way. I tried to guide the canoe to the far side, but it was no use and we drifted into the other canoes in the bend. Everybody was trying to get out of the entanglement without getting sunk. I was having a great time! I looked back at Clare, and she appeared in shock. I asked her what was wrong and somehow, she grabbed a sagging tree branch and started crying. I jumped out of the canoe into chest deep water with a strong current and told her to let go of the tree branch and I would push her and the canoe to the opposite shore. Apparently, she did not believe me, or she was just too scared. It took me several minutes to convince Clare to let go so I could take her to shore. After I got her to shore, I fished out our canoe and we finished our trip as planned. I had a great time and Clare apologized. I loved Clare very much and at times like these I even loved her more for being Clare.

Usually, Christmas was a private affair with Clare. Sometimes we would go to her moms for a small celebration after church service at St. Paul's Lutheran Church. We attended Church were we both grew up every Sunday and then would go to her mom's for lunch. We did that until our marriage started to fail. Then it seemed we stopped going to church or her mothers. I played Santa Clause for 2 Christmas' in 1974 and 1975 for my nieces and nephews at my sister Linda's house. It was a lot of fun. Everybody had a fun time and I liked giving out gifts to the kids.

1974 was the year we bought a new puppy. We did not have any kids so I thought this would be the next best thing. A friend of mine by the name of Dick Dye that worked at Elston Richards Storage Co. just had some full-blooded St. Bernard puppies and asked me if I would be interested in buying one from him. After looking the remaining pups, I picked out a miscolored one without a full mask. I got a discount because of her colors. The pup was the largest female of the litter. After Clare looked at her, she named the pup MUFFIN. Muffin grew up fast and within 6 months was full grown. She continued to grow until she was almost 200 pounds. She was a beautiful dog which at first was a blast to have around. Dick had told me that her mother was cross, and I guess I thought with a lot of lovin and attention our pup would not be mean but as she grew older, she became harder to manage. We eventually had to give her up to a farmer who lived near us.

1975 was the year we really started to travel in Ohio visiting all the neat places we could find, among them was the Warther Museum in Dover, The First Dental Museum in Bainbridge, the Gist Mill in Clifton, the Wright Patterson Air Base, the Wright Brothers Memorial also in Dayton, the Neal Armstrong Museum, The Thomas Edison Birthplace, The National Football League Hall of Fame in Akron, the Ohio Caverns, and all the state parks and monuments in Ohio.

It was late in 1975 when I met a new woman in my life by the name of Helen. My marriage with Clare was over but legally lasted for another 6 years. I felt that Clare was not ready for our separation and that I should stay around until she was ready to move on with her life. I had already made up my mind. We separated several times in the last 6 years. I am sure another woman in my life did not help, but it was something that just happened.

I did not have to look far because Helen Strahl was my boss's secretary. I was 29 and she was a cute 5'1 blonde that was 19 at the time. Several

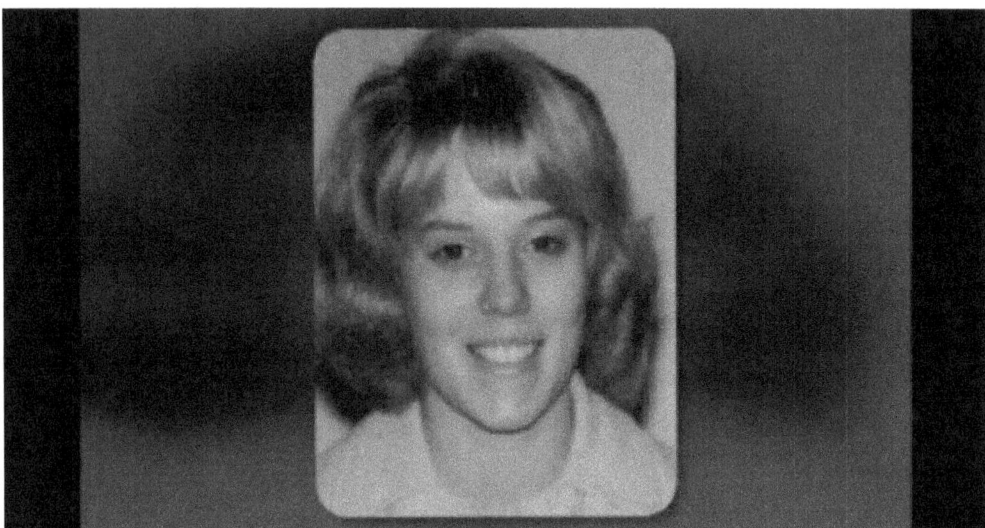
Helen

Photo by James Bruce

of the office people went out for a drink after work one day. As we were sitting around talking, Helen and I realized we both were looking for the same thing. I traveled between 3 warehouses, so I got to see Helen almost every day because she worked at the home office. Our home office was where I finished up my days' work and filed my reports. At first, we just talked and then we made a stop for a drink again just by ourselves. There were many times I really was hoping Clare and I could turn this thing around. One thing led to another before long we would stop at her apartment which led us making out and then making love. Helen and I had lots of fun together. I will never forget the time we went canoeing on a warm May day. The water was high, and the rapids were fast. She had never canoed before, and I had little experience. We were attempting to turn a curve in the waterway when a tree branch struck the canoe and tipped us over. In we went! Boy was that water COLD, and the warm May day became a cold, wet and bone chilling day and we had just started. We swam to shore, and I lost my wallet and Helen's camera. We recovered our canoe and finished out trip down the river without incident. We still had fun and kept each other warm.

Another time we played basketball in a light drizzle, but most of our time was spent at her apartment. Helen knew that I was a great big Elvis Presley fan, and she was too. Helen bought tickets for two (2) to see Elvis in Concert at the OSU French Field House and we both went to see the greatest entertainer in my life. It was without a doubt the best concert I have ever witnessed. We had an exciting time, and it will be something that I will never forget.

One time while we are resting in her bed after just making love, we heard a sound like someone was trying to get in the apartment door. I said, "what's that?' and Helen said, "it's probably the paper boy", when suddenly, a man was entering her apartment, so I jumped up naked and hid behind the bedroom door. Helen yelled to the man that she was with a friend, but it was too late he already headed to the room suggesting that it was nice finding

Helen sitting up in her bed naked with the sheet pulled up to her neck. Apparently, she gave someone a key to her apartment. Well, not hearing, Helen probably because after seeing Helen in her state of undress; he came into the room and sat down on her bed begging her to see him again. Helen said, "Bob I've got someone here," when she pointed across the room to me standing halfway behind the bedroom door naked!!! I just smiled and said, "Hi Bob."

To my surprise Bob said, "he was sorry" and left the apartment faster than when he came in. After he left, we just laughed, and Helen explained Bob to me and how they broke up, but he had kept bothering her. We took a shower together and went to the movies. Helen never heard from Bob again. We continued to see each other until June of 1976 when Clare and I took a vacation. I did not tell Helen that Clare and I were going on vacation.

In 1976 Clare and I took a vacation of all vacations when we traveled to the southwestern part of the United States visiting 17 states with stops at every national park, national monument, state park and unique location along the way.

I again planned stops at Carlsbad Caverns, White Sands National Monument, Grand Canyon National Park, Zion National Park, Arches National Park, Bryce Canyon National Park, Capital Reef National Park, and Petrified Forest National Park, Colorado National Monument, and the Royal Gorge.

Pictures by James Bruce

I had a great time, but it became too much for Clare. Not wanting to call it quits just yet, upon my return from vacation I called Helen. She was mad! She did not want to talk to me because I had not told her that I was going on vacation. She called me a couple of unmentionable names and hung up.

Eventually I had to decide and after 9 months with Helen I had decided that Clare and I should try yet again. I admitted my affair and told Clare I wanted to give it a try again. I remember crying like a baby, confused and ashamed. Helen told me she could not handle us not being together and decided to find work somewhere else. She called me a few times after that letting me know she was going to get married to a cop. I wished her well and told her I missed her, and I also told her that I might be getting a divorce. I was still very confused. She said if I did to give her a call.

Clare was working at Nationwide Insurance when we met and then took a job at Ashland Oil about the same time we got married. We did not make a lot of money, but we budgeted well and made a good living. Both of us got raises and promotions. After my second year with Elston Richards I was promoted to OS&D clerk which led me to Dock Supervisor in 1973 and OS&D Manager in 1974 and finally Personnel Manager in 1976 in charge of 3 offices and 37 women in those offices, payroll, office procedure and management for all three warehouses.

For about a year after that our marriage got better and I think we honestly tried to make it work, but as time wore on, we argued more and our affection for one another was clearly becoming very taxing.

Throughout the 1970's whenever Clare and I got a chance we would go and see a stage play. We both loved the Broadway shows, especially the musicals. Some of the shows I remember seeing included Show Boat, Oklahoma, I Do I Do, Oliver, The King and I, Cat on a Hot Tin Roof and Annie Get Your Gun. I always felt I was smarter than the average bear so one day I decided to take an IQ test offered by the Mensa International group and my score was 148 or as they said in the top 1% of the world's population.

In 1976 Lon Ferguson, Chuck Hewitt and I who loved to play golf together decided to go with a friend to a place called Fairfield Glade Resorts in Tennessee to play golf on a nationally recognized golf course and spend 3 days and 2 nights there. We loved the place, and the golf course was fantastic we decided together to buy a lot so we could continue to play on the course FREE there when we wanted to. We each paid $3000 for our share of the lot and continued to spend the next 6 years playing golf there. There was one problem when we bought the lot. Each of us failed to consult with our wives so that night, one by one, we each called our wives to let them know. We all felt better when that was over, and the wives seemed to go along with our decision.

Photo by James Bruce / **One of the par 3's at Fairfield Glade**

In 1979 Clare and I continued to travel whenever possible. In that year we decided to see another wonderful sight known as the Niagara Falls. Few natural spectacles rival the staggering beauty of Niagara Falls. Clare and I visited the Canadian side of the falls so we could see the Horseshoe Falls in its entirety.

Niagara Falls riverway started to
speed up as we got closer to the falls

We could see the mist ahead from the road
leading us to Niagara Falls

We got really close here to watch and feel
The power and beauty of the Niagara Falls

A postcard of the Niagara Falls in all its beauty
Being there was more exciting than any picture

Photos by James Bruce

This was my first visit to Canada and like Europe I really liked the cleanness of the places we visited and the friendly people.

In our last year of marriage Clare and I got up one morning and she went into the kitchen to clean. I went into my office located in the spare bedroom to work. Suddenly, I heard a scream and two thumps. I yelled for Clare, she moaned and tried to respond, so I jumped up and ran into the kitchen where I found Clare laying in the middle of the floor shaking and bleeding from the head. I quickly grabbed a towel to stop the bleeding and grabbed Clare to try to help her. I had seen a couple of seizures before so I knew how to help making sure her throat passage was clear so she could breathe ok, and comfort her until the emergency squad could get there. She could not breathe so I pried opened her mouth with my fingers and looked inside to see that she had swallowed her tongue. She was turning blue so I very quickly, without hesitation, put my fingers in her mouth to pull her tongue back so she could breathe. It worked, she started to breathe but the pain from her biting my fingers made it tough to stay in that position, but I did, and her skin color came back to near normal and she was breathing normal again, so I let go and helped her to her feet and led her to the couch where she collapsed and appeared to go to sleep. Still scared I immediately ran to the phone and called the emergency squad. When I went back to check on Clare she awoke screaming as if I was a stranger. This really startled me, and it was then that I realized that she did not know me. She kept saying repeatedly asking "who I was." A few minutes later she got up, ran into the bathroom, and locked the door. I was waiting at the door for the squad. The squad arrived and we started by trying to tell Clare that they were here to help and wanted to take her to the Madison County Hospital to be checked out. She eventually agreed to go, and I followed her to the hospital. After many trips to the doctor, they diagnosed her as being an epileptic. It is a condition that apparently just reappeared according to her mother. I never knew she had any physical problems until then.

The movies provided us with Billy Jack, Dirty Harry, The Godfather, The Poseidon Adventure, Deliverance, The Exorcist, Papillon, The Towering Inferno, Jaws, and One Flew Over the Cuckoo's Nest. The music featured Rod Stewart, The Osmonds, Cher, Santana, America, Elton John, Jim Croce, The O'Jays, Lynyrd Skynyrd, and The Captain and Tennille. Television amused us with All in The Family, Laverne and Shirley, Sanford and Sons, Happy Days, The Jeffersons, The Waltons, The Mary Tyler Moore Show, Little House on the Prairie, Sonny and Cher, and Monday Night Football. The Events of the time included Apollo XIV Lands on the Moon; Vietnam is Over, President Nixon Resigns and Jimmy Hoffa disappears.

Let the Games Begin

In the spring of 1975, I was invited to help coach a youth baseball team by John Bradford who was the head coach of the Cardinals. The Cardinals were a youth baseball team that was a part of the West Jefferson Youth Athletic Association. At the time John and I both worked for Elston Richards Storage Company. A few games into the season John's son decided that he did not want to play so I took over the team. I had a good team, and we went on the win the title for our division with a score of 1-0 and played in the championship which we lost 5-0. We took the kids to see the Clippers (AAA Yankee farm team) that summer where they got to meet one of my baseball idols, Mickey Mantle.

For several years we also took them to baseball training camps held by the Columbus Clippers. During the Labor Day weekend each year West Jefferson celebrates that weekend by cooking a giant ox in a pit in the ground and providing the community with a parade, games, and amusement rides at the local park behind the old Jr. High School. Of course, the highlight is the Ox Roast Sandwiches served the last day of the celebration. This is a time when the community organizations get together creating games of chance so that we can raise money for our charity.

It is a wonderful time for all, and I really enjoyed the chance to help the community and my favorite organization the West Jefferson Youth Athletic Association. I attended, organized, and participated in this annual event for 8 years. It was a lot of fun working with friends, members, and parents of the children in the community.

Coaching was a lot of fun, and it gave me some free time away from Clare. It was coaching the kids that I really enjoyed. The kids would do the funniest things. Some of the things I remember was when I was coaching the Cardinals, I was looking for one of the kids that was supposed to be playing 3rd Base and I found him playing in the sand behind the back stop. On another team I had this boy who was playing in the outfield when he decided he had to go to the bathroom, so he just turned his back to the crowd and peed while the game was going on and laughing the whole time. Everybody else was too. There were several times that after a hit the kids would start to run to 3rd instead of 1st or not run at all or get to a base and not know what to do next. But you know the simple joys of the kids was what it was all about. The kid's laughs, their faces when they got their first hit or home run, or their first catch. I wondered if I really wanted to grow up. That fall I was invited to help coach a youth football team with Lew Workman, a policeman. We named the team the Vikings. The Vikings won the Championship that year with a record of 5-0-1

One year while coaching baseball I took my baseball team to a Columbus Clippers (AAA Yankee organization) summer training camp. Catcher Training.

Without a doubt while coaching the greatest experience was taking the team to see one of my baseball idols Mickey Mantle. That's one of my kids getting their baseball signed by Mickey.

That's the pitching coach of the Columbus Clippers teaching the kids how to hold the ball while pitching.

Photos by

James Bruce

That's John Bradford and I coaching the Cardinals in 1975
We won the National League Championship

Jimmy Dean the Sausage King
and Country Entertainer being
introduced at Clippers Game

The San Diego Chicken entertaining
Us at a Columbus Clippers Game

Enjoyed 8 years helping raise money for the WJYAA
At the West Jefferson Ox Roast 1975-1982

Photos by James Bruce

That winter I was voted to be President of the West Jefferson Youth Athletic Association for 1976 and reelected in 1977-1978 and 1979. I also coached my first youth basketball team along with Jack Wamsley and we won the

championship going undefeated the entire season. The name of the team was the Lakers. By this time, I really loved being involved in this!!!

As President of the youth athletic association, I decided to add more teams and programs to the existing ones. At that time, we had 4 boys' baseball teams, 4 boys' football teams and 6 boys' basketball teams. I went to the schools in the community in 1977 and worked with them on signing up new kids for the programs. It was a remarkable success story and we ended with doubling up on all the sports' teams.

Next came the girl's program which I introduced by adding a girls' basketball program in 1978. Girls Basketball was totally unheard of at that time. It also was a remarkable success! Lon Ferguson, and I coached the Celtics which also went undefeated that year. The next year 1979 I opened 3rd and 4th grade boys' and girls' basketball and a t-ball baseball program for the boys. I ended up coaching a 3rd and 4th grade girls' basketball team also called the Lakers. We went undefeated that year as well.

I was approached by several women about softball, so I also started a 5th and 6th softball program for girls. The following year in 1980 a couple of dads came to me wanting to start a boys and girls soccer program. Max, Jerry Doran, and I went to a soccer coaching and umpire school in Columbus to learn how to start a soccer program. When we finished the classes, we went to work creating an extraordinarily successful soccer league. All the while I was commissioner of several of the programs and even coached several teams either as a head or assistant coach. I also umpired or was a referee of all sports at many, many games.

Banquets were held after each program where we would hand out trophies and share in a potluck style dinner and as Commissioner of many sports, I was responsible for the arrangements. Each coach would introduce their team and award each player for their season. I really enjoyed the smiles on all those kids' faces.

Yet another parent by the name of Bev Loughridge came to me with an idea that we should own the community recreation center where we played all the kid's basketball games. At the time we were having trouble playing in the community center owned and managed by the West Jefferson Township Trustees. One time the trustees were thinking about closing the center because it needed repair and they did not have the money to fix it up. In doing so the kids in the community would have no place to play basketball. At the time we were taking signups for boys 3-4-5-6 grades, and girls 3-4-5-6 grades with at least 8 teams each. That is a lot of kids. So, the next meeting the township trustees had I sent out a message to all the parents that we needed their support. On a night, when usually 6-8 people showed up the entire gym was totally packed. We got our point across and succeeded in keeping the gym. I represented the WJYAA at the meeting in a small meeting room next to the gym while the people supporting the program waited for the outcome. After the meeting I told the supporters of the outcome and there was a huge ovation. Everybody went home happy, including me.

I even helped coach volleyball
which I knew very little about
but enjoyed anyway.

At the age of 41 that me playing
in a coached game (middle) 1987

Some of the kids of West Jefferson with John Galbraith (second
from the right) at the dedication for the recreation center
he bought and donated to the village

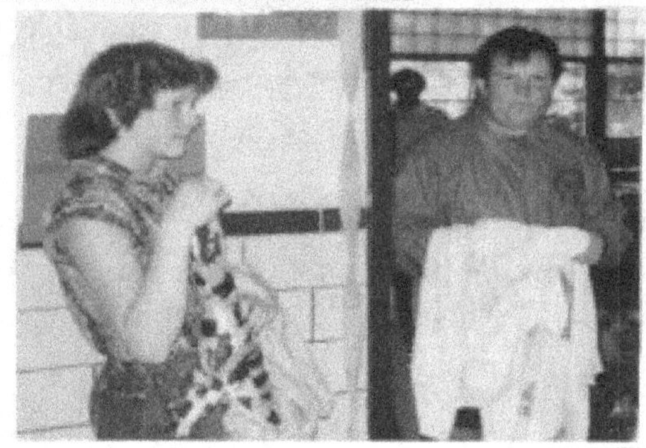

I soaked at a fun raiser at the local elementary school where
the kids threw water balloons at me. Successfully I might add.

Photos by James Bruce

After that meeting, Bev Loughridge contacted John Galbreath on a cold call about buying the gym for us. John at the time was one of the richest men in the USA and owned the Pittsburgh Pirates, plus many, many real estate interests in the US. He was the owner of past Kentucky Derby winners. To my surprise John invited Bev and I to his house for a meeting. Bev contacted me and asked me if I would go along. When we got to his house which was located on his estate halfway between Columbus and West Jefferson known as Darby Dan Farms. (Named after his son Dan) and located on Darby Creek. We were escorted to the main house where we discussed the events, the gym and its condition, and the kids. We met in his great room where he gave us a tour of the trophies he had received, pictures and stories of meetings with the famous people the world over included Queen Elizabeth.

He showed us some of the rest of his house and where Bing Cosby and Bob Hope stayed in his guest houses. He wanted to know about us and when I told him I was an insurance and real estate agent he advised me to concentrate on one and I would do better in life.

We later met John along with the Mayor of West Jefferson to show him the gym and its condition. After the showing he advised us to come up with a plan and we should have another meeting and that he would help. After meetings with the mayor, we decided that the community might be interested in supporting the repairs if Mr. Galbraith would be interested in buying the center. We took our plan to Mr. Galbraith. At the meeting there was Bev, Myself, the Mayor, and a Trustee representing the owners. After greetings and introductions, we got down to business at hand not knowing what to expect. Everybody there expressed thanks and was wondering if Mr. Galbreath would help. Without hesitation Mr. Galbreath pointed to the trustee and asked him how much they would want for the building. HE HAD NO IDEA. My heart sunk to the bottom of my chest. Mr. Galbreath asked him what he thought it was worth. The trustee suggested the building would need lots of repair to make it saleable. Mr. Galbreath said "I give you $10,000 if the community would invest $10,000 or repair the building looking at the mayor. He sincerely wanted to help the kids and I think he would have doubled that but to my surprise everybody agreed and shook hands.

It was not over with yet. We had to convince both the town trustees and governing body of West Jeff. I went to both meetings. We eventually came to an agreement. Thanks to a lot of people, lots of work and of course, Mr. Galbreath. For the time being we had a place for the kids to play for as long as the building will stand. I understand the building was torn down much later but used for many years as suggested.

I had a great time and I think everybody associated with the programs did too, especially the kids! That was what it was all about. One year I helped the local Jaycees at a swimming meet as a judge. That fall I commissioned a successful shoot, pass and dribble basketball program as sponsored and promoted by the National Basketball Association (NBA) called Hot Shots. I promoted it through the schools and the youth athletic association, and we had a great turnout. For the next two years I organized a local track meet sponsored by the local Jaycees. I took the winners of the track meets to 2 state meets one near Akron and one in Granville, Ohio on separate occasions. Everybody involved had a fun time, especially the kids.

Here I was asked to be a judge at the local swimming meet put on by the West Jefferson Jaycees. (Gray shirts and white socks)

For two years I was asked to Commission a local Jaycee Track Meet and the winner went on to the State Finals.

Here's a few of kids from my team at our house for some R&R. Clare is on the left. This is my only picture I have of Clare

Photos by James Bruce

In 1978, I was nominated and won the Outstanding Young Man Award by the United States Jaycees as nominated by the West Jefferson Jaycees for my work with the kids in that community.

I also was the Commissioner for a basketball program called Shoot, Pass and Dribble for the West Jefferson Jaycees. The winners on the left and that me keeping score of the shooting competition on the right.

Pack 121 scouts receive award

Cub Scout Pack 121 had its blue and gold banquet Saturday night at the West Jefferson Middle School auditorium.

About 300 persons attended, including honored guests Jeff Martin, southwest district executive; Jim Bruce, assistant district commissioner for Madison County; and Rev Dale Gensler of United Methodist Church in West Jefferson.

"Duncan, the Magician" entertained the audience with his wit and magical talent. Cub master Paul Woods presented trophies, plaques and awards earned by the scouts throughout the year.

The banquet was concluded with the presentation of the Arrow of Light award to Dustin Desarro, Chase Adkins and Larry Hinkle. The Arrow of Light is the highest award that can be earned

in cub scouting. Also, it is the only cub scout award that can be worn on the Boy Scout uniform.

The West Jefferson scout program has 91 members and 14 leaders who provide leadership for the cubs.

HELPING Duncan the Magician in a magic act are Vince Melfi, left, and Richie Holcomb.

I joined the Boy Scouts when I was 10 years old and I always wanted to be a scout leader, but that never happened until I was asked by the Madison County Commissioner if I would Like to help as an Assistant District Commissioner which I did in 1982. I really enjoyed my short tenure and was glad I could help.

Photos by James Bruce

In 1982 I was asked if I could help with the boy scouts' program by the District Commissioner for Madison County. I told him that I was extremely busy but since I was 10 years old when I first joined the scouts, I have always wanted to be a scout leader. He suggested that I be his assistant and help with the local special meetings in his absence. I agreed and attended whenever I could. A lot of the kids I coached or had coached were in the scouts and they were glad to see me.

I was glad I could help. Probably the greatest accolade I ever received was when the students in a 7th grade class were asked to write about a famous person they knew. Seven (7) of the kids in the English class of about 30 wrote about me. I now think about all the people that helped make those programs a success and I can honestly say that took literally 100's of parents and friends that ran or helped run those programs. Without them all of what I accomplished would not have been possible. I was 32 years old.

I loved coaching sports to the kids I totally involved myself in the West Jefferson Youth Athletic Association from 1975-1982. I coached Boys Basketball grades 3-6, Girls Basketball grades 3-6, Boys Football one year as an assistant, Boys Baseball grades 3-6, Girls Softball grades 5-6, Girls Volleyball as an assistant and Boys Soccer. I also umpired and refereed all sports. I was the Commissioner for Basketball and Baseball during that period. I with the help of a lot of parents and friends I started the Girls Basketball, Girls Softball, Girls Volleyball, and the Soccer program. With the help of the West Jefferson Schools, I also extended the grades in all sports to add more children to their programs. Here are some of the teams I coached.

Robin and I coached our first and my last sports team in Volleyball.

We coached the Lakers to another undefeated season again.

Photos by James Bruce

I was the assistant coach for Chastity's (#6 on the lower right) first T-ball team for the Westland Youth Athletic Association.

Jim and Carol Bickler (coaches) coached the Pirates 5th and 6th grade in Softball

Photos by James Bruce

n assistant coach of the soccer team Chad was on standing of me.

Photos by James Bruce

I was later asked by Carol Bickler, the West Jefferson Jr. High Coach, if I would like to coach Gymnastics for her younger daughter which I agreed to. We decided to open the class for any that would be interested. 137 kids signed up!!! I retired from coaching after that.

Lon (R)and I (middle) coaching our undefeated 5th and 6th Girls basketball team.

Lon and I handing out the awards For the Champions

This is a photo of the entire team Taken at the Awards Banquet Coached by Jim Bruce and Lon Ferguson

Photos by James Bruce

My New Careers

I attended Wittenberg University from 1973 to 1978 as a part time student at times putting in enough hours to be considered a full-time student so I applied for and was granted a letter of admission to Wittenberg University with a 3.0 grade point average. I never finished my schooling at Wittenberg but before I left, I took the mandatory courses in Real Estate to get my Real Estate License. One of the kids I was coaching had a dad that was the Real Estate Broker and Owner for Frank B Young Realtors. His name was Richard Clark. Dick was the one that suggested that I take the real estate courses so that I could sale real estate for his company. I agreed to give it a try. I took the test for my real estate license and passed with a near perfect score. I quit Elston Richards Storage Company after 7 years with the company in 1977 to pursue a real estate career.

IN 1976 WHILE AT ELSTON Richards Storage Company I started helping friends and family with a tax preparation service. Eventually evolving into a part time business known as Bruce Tax and Accounting. A service I terminated in 2017.

Realtor of the Year

Jan Rhodes (front, left) receives the Realtor of the Year plaque from Dick Clark, president of Frank B. Young Realtors. Mrs. Rhodes won the firm's award for her sales and service during 1978. In back are Dick Grant (left), Dave Moody and Jim Bruce, all awarded monthly awards last year.

Photos by James Bruce

I started my real estate career in May of 1977 and for the first 6 months I spent learning the business and did not sale one piece of real estate until I sold a vacant lot at Lake Choctaw for $2000 in November of that year. Way to go Jim!!! Things got better and by the spring of 1978 I was a leading real estate salesman at Frank B Young during 1978 and 1979. In late 1979 while at Frank B. Young the owner and broker Dick Clark knew of my building background and suggested that I build a few houses for him. I decided to form a partnership with my bother Cliff. I would be the General Contractor and Cliff would oversee construction. We decided the partnership would be named C&J Builders.

Photo by James Bruce

Cliff Bruce

From 1979 through 1981 Cliff and I built a total of 7 homes at Lake Choctaw and completed numerous remodeling projects until the interest rates dried up the construction business forcing us to close shop and look for other employment. About that time the interest rates started climbing to an all-time high and the real estate market dropped out of sight.

A good friend of mine by the name of Ray Stischok that was also an agent/broker at Frank B Young suggested that I give the Insurance Business a try. At the time he was preparing to move into that line of business with the Metropolitan Life Insurance Company. It sounded like something I might be interested in, so I met with Ray and Company reps to sign up. After an interview I was accepted and sent to school in Dayton, Ohio to become an Insurance Agent for Metropolitan Life. It was 1982 and I kept my real estate license active for an occasional sale and entered the insurance business. My marriage with Clare was over and I was starting a new career. Clare and I were divorced in 1981 after 10 years of marriage. I am sorry I never called Helen. Helen died in 2019.

We sold our house and Clare moved to Columbus to be closer to her work. I heard she later re-married and moved to New Jersey. I hoped she found happiness. At the time I stayed in our house until the new owners moved in. After our house sold, I moved into another new house a partnership of Lon Ferguson, Chuck Hewitt and I owned that was under construction. Later I moved to a little house my parents owned in West Jefferson.

I started selling Insurance for Metropolitan Life in 1981 and at first, I was doing extremely well selling enough Life and Casualty Insurance to be named to the Top Five Salesmen in the District. I received a plaque and was hosted to dinner at a top restaurant with the other 4 salesmen by the President of Metropolitan Life in Dayton. The meal was good but my time at Met was short lived. I kept my license active with an occasional sale of casualty insurance as an independent agent doing business as Bruce Insurance.

Late that year I decided to get in the sporting goods business. It is something I just wanted to do, and I thought I would be successful at it with all the local experience I had in sports. With all the other things I was doing at the time I thought I needed a partner and a good friend of mine and fellow coach by the name of Mike Kay also thought it might be a clever idea to open a sporting goods store in West Jefferson, so we agreed to try it. Mike and I decided to open the store right before football season because we knew with the accounts, we could garner at that time of the year would work out well. Everything worked as planned but after a few months Mike decided that it was not for him and so I decided to go it alone. Jim's and Mike's store became known as JB Sporting Goods. The first thing I did was move the location to a store site to Main Street in West Jefferson and purchase additional goods for the store.

Robin and I

I met Robin Hendrickson through a friend by the name of Bill Pettit. Robin was 23 years old at the time a single mother of 2 children that needed a job to help cover expenses for her custody battle and I thought I could help. She was already working 2 jobs but was looking for another part time job and the position I had available would work out well with her except she did not have a car and needed transportation to my sporting goods store. Robin was living with Bill Pettit and his family at the time. It was here that I met my 2nd wife Robin Marie Bruce.

Again, with all the things I was doing I did not really have the time to run the store so I asked my parents (both being retired) if they would be interested in helping and they offered to invest in the store. I offered them 50% ownership for 50% invested monies. They agreed and immediately helped to improve and manage the store which at first went well. As my parents took more control, I was less interested in the daily operations so I decided that I would take a back seat as they invested more money eventually owning 90%. At that point I had basically lost control of the store and decided to look for another job. The store did not work out for my parents either. They wanted to open their own store in London, Ohio nearer where they lived. Since all the merchandise and debt of JB Sporting Goods was in my name I had to file bankruptcy.

Robin and I would ride back and forth from Bill's house and the sporting goods store several times a week. It was here that I got to know Robin and I really felt she just needed a little help. Robin's two kids Chasity and Chad were living with their fathers' mother at the time. Since my divorce from Clare, I had dated several times and up until I met Robin, I had not found anyone interesting enough to spend time with. I did not know it then, but I was looking at my second wife and the love of my life. I had been single for 2 years and although I was always looking for a wife I was in no hurry. I do not remember what I was looking for but at first, I knew it was not Robin either or so I thought.

Jim and Robin's Portrait Photo 1984

Photo by James Bruce

During our time together we talked a lot about her kids and the tough times she had during her life losing her father to cancer when she was just 3 and her mother being shot to death by her stepfather when she was only 14. She also told me about her first marriage and how it did not work out, but her two children were the pride of her life. She was working to get custody of her children and job stability was one factor and a place to live on her own was another. She worked hard at times working for 3 companies at one time. She worked at McDonalds, Bobby Layman's Auto and at an ice cream parlor while occasionally working for me. I was really impressed. She found a lovely place to live that was subsidized and as we got closer that wonderful place became OUR wonderful place, but not until I met her kids.

I was invited to move in with Bill Pettit and his family where Robin also stayed. The more time I spent with Robin I realized I liked what this girl was all about. We did not have a lot of money, so we started dating by spending more time together at Bill's Place. Other dates included trips to the local Laundromat whenever we needed to wash our clothes. At other times we would go to a nearby White Castle burger joint for an inexpensive meal. It sounds silly but it was these times that we still remember as loving time spent together.

Things started heating up after that when on one occasion we camped out in a tent in Bill's back yard. I was anxious and Robin was scared to the point she faked an orgasm and since I was let us say "experienced" in these things I asked her why she faked it and she said she was scared and thought it was the right thing to do at the time. Later we both settled down and made up for it and this time it was not fake. We were in Love.

Robin and I had decided to move shortly after that into her new apartment, but I was not on the lease and technically not allowed to stay with her because it was an apartment for only her and the kids.

Photo by Classic Cars

While I was still living in West Jefferson and Robin was still at Bill's place, she was court ordered to go to ex-husbands mothers place and pick up the kids, but she did not have a vehicle to go. I knew how much she wanted to see her kids because I knew she had not seen them in almost a year. I told her to take my old beat-up Volkswagen. I was afraid she might not make it there and back. I tried to get her a rental but that did not work. So off she went in my beat-up old Volkswagen that barely ran with only one door that worked. I prayed that she would make it up there and back, but she did not care. She was on her way up the pickup her kids. I was so glad I could help, that tears came from feeling so happy for her. They made it back and I was introduced to Chasity and Chad. Chasity was 5 and Chad was 2 and we hit it off immediately especially with Chad.

Photos by James Bruce

Chad and Chasity

Chasity, being a little bit older, was not sure who I was or what I was doing with her mommy. She kept asking when mommy and daddy were getting back together again and who was this guy named Jim. The kids where neat but the clothes they were wearing needed cleaned so badly that I decided at once that I was going to go buy them some new clothes to wear. I left without telling anybody and returned with some new clothes for them to wear. Now it was Robin's turn to cry, and I was glad to help. Robin gave them a bath and put on their new clothes. It was then that I knew this was going to be my new family.

Robin took them back to their grandmothers and upon her return we planned our new life together. We got married in October of 1982 at the Franklin County Courthouse in the judge's office along with a little 3-year-old by the name of Chad. The whole time Chad hugged his new dad's leg which the judge got a kick out of. After we were married, he wished us well and told me to take loving care of that little guy. Robin got permanent custody of the kids and we settled down to raising a family.

When I met Chas and Chad, they were 5 and 2 respectively and when Robin and I got married they had just turned were 6 and 3. I always wanted a family and I thought I would be a good dad. Clare and I never had any children. My new family was what my life was missing. I loved being a dad and there was no greater feeling than bringing smiles and laughter to their little faces. I treated the kids just as if they were mine. One of the greatest moments I will ever cherish was when these two kids call me DAD. We all had a great life together.

That first year together I will never forget their first birthday party, it was the time that we spent in the Darby Creek Metropolitan Park and flew a kite, their first trip to see the Easter Bunny and of course our first Christmas together. In summer of 1983 we took a trip to the Ohio State Fair for the kid's first adventure to a state fair. Robin, Chasity, Chad, and I really enjoyed our time at the fair and the kids especially enjoyed the rides.

Our first Christmas together

Chad and Chas on a ride at
The Ohio State Fair 1983

Chas on another ride at
The fair

Chad on a train ride
At the fair

Chasity, Jessie Warner my sister
Brenda's son and Chad

Photos by James Bruce

My favorite song that year was Maneater by Daryl Hall and John Oates. Our favorite movie was ET but at first it scared Chad. Robin liked An Officer and a Gentleman. Among the events that year were a gallon of gas cost

$1.30, actor John Belushi died of drugs, Cd's were new, and AIDS was a new mysterious disease. It was 1982 and I was 36 years old.

From 1978 thru 1982 the music heard over the airwaves included such songs from Queen, Abba, Eric Clapton, Exile, Blondie, the Village People, Charlie Daniels, Kim Carnes, Air Supply, Daryl Hall and John Oates, Kool and the Gang and Journey. It was a fun time at the movies which included Grease, Animal House, Superman, Apocalypse Now, 9 to 5, Airplane, Raiders of the Lost Ark, Porkys, Stripes, ET, Tootsie, and An Officer and a Gentleman. Television got a little more serious with 60 minutes, but also included shows like Mork and Mindy, All in the Family, Taxi, Soap, Dallas, One Day at a Time, Love Boat, Threes Company, Different Strokes and The A Team. The events during this time included an accident at 3 Mile Island's Nuclear Plant which threatened the area, Washington's Mt. Saint Helen erupted, John Lennon was shot to death in New York City, Ronald Reagan inaugurated as the 40th President, and Prince Charles and Lady Diana marry.

New Directions

I closed the sporting goods store and decided that I wanted to look for a better job. Owning a sporting goods store in a small town of 6000 people just did not make a lot of sense or money. I had a family now and I needed to get to work and provide for them. I first tried a sales position at Color Tile and at the same time joined the Army Reserves for one year. The sales position at Color Tile was eliminated by new management and was let go or fired since I would not sign a paper saying I quit. They figured that they would not have to pay me unemployment if I signed, but I knew better. I received unemployment while I was looking for another position.

In 1983 with my real estate background, I applied for a position of mortgage loan officer at the Norwest Mortgage Company. 25 people applied for the job and after a review and interview process, I was picked as their new loan officer. The next year Norwest decided to close their Columbus office and I interviewed and was accepted for the same position at the Priority Mortgage Company in Worthington.

At the time Norwest closed their office down I had over 1 million dollars in mortgage loans on the books and they agreed to pay us our commission for all closings that followed. I did not receive my commission as scheduled so I called Norwest's primary office in Cincinnati, Ohio. I told them that I had not been paid my commissions and they asked me how many loans I had made and when I told them the person, I was talking to said "if you had that much on the books, we would not have closed!" I kept all my records of the mortgage applications taken so I sent him copies of them. He apologized and wanted to know if I wanted to relocate to Cincinnati. They sent me my commission checks as promised.

In 1984 I started at Priority my closing ratio was low at about 50% and my income gradually increased with more experience. By the time I left Priority at the end of my second year my closing ratio was about 93% and I grossed over $84,000 dollars that year. The money was good but the pressure to handle that many cases got to me, and my health started to decline. I had several anxiety attacks, so I went to see a doctor and he told me I had to find another job or die.

By this time both kids were in school, and I was for the first time in my life a proud husband and parent to two of the most wonderful kids in the whole wide world. 1984 was our first family vacations we all enjoyed one to Walt Disney World and the other one Robin and I took alone to Niagara Falls.

On the way to Disney World, we made several stops, one was at the Air Force Museum in Dayton Ohio which was interesting. I had visited the Museum before, but this was Robin's and the kids first time. It was a fun time, and we had not even left Ohio. I have always wanted to see St. Augustine, the oldest fort in the United States and visit the city that has the oldest school building.

Jim Chas and Chad in front
of a jet at the Air Force Museum

Our first stop on this vacation was
At the Air Force Museum in Dayton

A postcard photo of the oldest fort in the USA called St. Augustine

We entered the fort through this drawbridge and we played on the
beaches all along the ocean front down to Daytona, Florida.

Photos by James
Bruce

This was the rail tram we took to different parts of Disney World
such as the photo of a Colonial Area to the right

A couple of pictures of Main Street USA Disney World style were
we did some shopping and eat lunch and dinner.

A card photo taken at night of the castle located near Main Street

Photos by James Bruce

Chas Chad and Robin
in Florida

5 photos of Chas and Chad enjoying the rides and special creatures at Disney World in Florida

Photos by James Bruce

Robin and I took this outside elevator to the top of the tower

A view of the American Falls from the Rooftop of the Tower

A view of the Horseshoe Falls from the Rooftop of the Tower

While in Canada we visited some of The towns nearby

This postcard shows what we saw at the Allegany State Park in northwestern part of New York on a stop while going home.

Photos by James Bruce

Of course, we stopped and took the complete tour of the fort, the city, and the beaches.

Photos by James Bruce

Our next stop was at Marineland in Florida where we got to see several performances and visit throughout the park. It was not as big as Sea World but clean and professionally presented. We had an exciting time, and the kids had a blast. We stopped at Gatorland Zoo where we got to see all kinds of gators and other water creatures, but probably the neatest thing was when it was feeding time. They served the gators their favorite meal which was whole chickens served from a drawn line and by hand. Chad and Chas even got to ride a giant turtle.

Another fun time and we still have not got to Disney. I rented a Condo at Disney World which was located close to everything, especially the park. We spent 2 days enjoying all the rides and amusements we could which started by taking a tram to the main area of the park. We got to see a Disney Parade which included Mickey and Minnie Mouse a favorite for all of us kids including mom and dad. This was possibly the best 2 days a family could have, and we did in this fantasy land that Walt built. Thanks to you Walt Disney.

Photo by https://en.wikipedia.org/wiki/Walt_Disney

A stop at the Gatorland Zoo was exciting and the kids really enjoyed entrance

This is the turtle the kids rode.

This was a close up of the live alligators sunning and resting

The most exciting time at the zoo was feeding time for the alligators. Whole chickens was on their memu. Gators can jump.

Photos by James Bruce

Robin and I decided later that year to also take another vacation without Chad and Chasity to Niagara Falls spending most of our time on the Canadian side. I had been to Niagara Falls with my first wife so I had an idea what we should see and do while there. The weather was beautiful, and the falls were fantastic. Once we got there, we spent a lot of time taking in all the sights and sounds. We took a walk along the walkway that followed the river after the falls. We spent some time taking in the sight of the Horseshoe and American Falls. The current along the river was a remarkable sight with rapids faster and higher than anything I have ever seen. We also took the tramway across the river, rode the Maid of the Mist; a boat that took us right up to the falls. The experience of riding The Maid of the Mist right up to the falls was an experience that we will not forget. The power of both the boat and the falls left me with an awe-inspiring respect and a feeling of wonder. Our next stop was to ride an "outside the building" elevator to the top of Panasonic Tower where Robin and I dined on stuffed flounder. Robin had never eaten out at anything fancier than Long John Silvers so this was a real treat for her. The restaurant was at the top of the tower, and it rotated as you ate so you saw a panoramic view of the falls area. When we started to eat our meal, Robin stopped eating and whispered to me that her fish had not been cleaned!!! I looked at it and just laughed. The fish was stuffed with Spinach and Shrimp!!! While we were on the Canadian side, we also took some time to visit the surrounding countryside and some local parks. On the way back home from falls, I couldn't help myself and we stopped at the pretty Allegany State Park located in southwestern New York. It was a great trip, and I looked forward to many more adventures with Robin during our marriage.

In 1985 we moved from our apartment to our first house we bought located at 112 Chester Street in West Jefferson, Ohio in a town where I had my real estate office. It was a 2 story with 2 bedrooms and 2 baths with high ceilings and large rooms. The living room was 40 by 14, a classic Victorian style. The property needed a lot of work, but I thought it was a good buy at $36,000 dollars. Robin and I worked hard fixing it up and over 3 years we spent over 12,000 dollars on improvements. I bought it with 3-year balloon, so we had to sale it or pay it off. Several other real estate deals were falling apart so we sold it for $47,900 dollars and rented a nice house on the next block in the year 1988.

One of our travels for 1985 again took us south through Kentucky and Tennessee. This time we also took Rita, a sister of Robin's. Our first stop was at the Kentucky Horse Farm where we greeted with a statue of Man O War, one of the greatest horses of all time.

Kentucky Horse Park and Cumberland Falls / Photos by James Bruce

We toured the farm and took in all its history with a large buggy ride around the farm. Our next stop was another

stop at Cumberland Falls   Photo by
James Bruce

and Mammoth Caves National Park.

Photo by National Park Service

This time we took a different tour of the Caves which took us through many new areas and challenges. One area took us through an area known as fat mans squeeze. Rita, being a large woman barely made it through! She almost got stuck and gave everybody a good laugh including Rita. At the end of the cave tour, we encountered a stairway to an upper level which took you up to dizzying heights including me. I was glad that part of the tour was over which was a physical challenge as well.

Later that year the entire family took another trip to Tennessee. Our goal was to visit The Lost Sea another unique cave system that featured an underground lake of water.

Photo by Bing.com/Images

The Group photo of the tourist that took the tour of the Lost Sea 1986

Photo by James Bruce

We took a boat ride on the lake and while we on the lake we were told that there was fish in the lake, and we could feed the fish while there. The tour guide gave us dog food to feed the fish and they attacked the pebbles like piranha. We also were told the fish living in the bottom of the cave did not have eyes, because it was completely dark except when the tourists arrive. After that we took in all the sites in Chattanooga's area such as Ruby Falls, the Incline Railway, and Black Water Falls State Park. We finished with a quick stop in Nashville.

Incline Railway Ruby Falls

Photo by https://en.wikipedia.org/wiki/Lookout_Mountain_Incline_Railway

Ruby Falls Photo by Getsready.com

We really enjoyed Ruby Falls yet another cave system that featured a real fall deep inside the caves. The Ruby Falls entrance was located at the top of a mountain that offered a magnificent view of the basin south of Chattanooga from several vistas. Another stop was a ride down a mountain top via a railway known as the Incline Railway the steepest one in the world. Next was one of the most beautiful State Parks I have ever seen in the country known as Black Water Falls State Park where we saw several different waterfalls from different heights. We crossed one of the creeks via a suspension bridge where Robin had to stop and balance herself several times because it was swaying too much. This is when I found out Robin was afraid of heights. Everybody had to help and encourage her to cross the bridge.

In 1986, I pondered on what else I wanted to do and decided to take a position as Senior Loan Officer at the Ohio State Mortgage Company, a smaller mortgage company with a whole lot less stress. One of my mortgage loan clients was a man by the name of Mike Snyder who owned the Snyder Insurance Agency. Mike and I hit it off right away and I told him I was licensed to sell insurance in Ohio. He asked if I would like to be an agent with his firm. That year I started selling casualty insurance part time for the Snyder Insurance Agency.

In 1987 I decided to test for my Real Estate Brokers License and passed with a near perfect score. I was back in the Insurance and Real Estate business this time as owner/broker. Bruce Real Estate and Insurance opened for business in 1987. My insurance business grew and by 1988 I was at a point where I had to relocate my agency with Mikes where I sold insurance under the Snyder Insurance name. It was located in Grandview a suburb of Columbus. My real estate office was in West Jefferson.

1987 was another momentous year of travels which included a second trip to the beautiful Luray Caverns of Virginia, the Blue Ridge Parkway and a first time stop to Chimney Rock Park, Grandfather's Mountain and Mount Mitchell. Later that year we decided to go to see the home of the greatest entertainer in the world during my life a stop to see Graceland home of Elvis Presley in Memphis, Tennessee.

The largest and most beautiful cave in Virginia is Luray Caverns nestled in the banks of the Blue Ridge Mountains.

The new entrance to Luray Caverns

The old entrance to Luray Caverns

That's Jim and Donnie Sherman in his fishing boat.

A photo of the stairway we took to Luray Cavern's lower level

Another view from Blue Ridge Pkwy

Photos by James Bruce

Luray Cavern is, in fact, Eastern America's largest and most popular caverns. A U.S. Natural Landmark noted for the profuse variety of formations and natural color. From well-lighted, paved walkways we explored cathedral sized rooms with ceilings 10 stories high, filled with towering stone columns and crystal-clear pools. While in the Caverns we heard the haunting sounds of the world's only Stalacpipe Organ. In addition, at Luray Caverns, we experienced the history of America in an exhibit featuring over 140 items relating to transportation including cars, carriages, coaches, and costumes from 1725. From there we rode the beautiful Blue Ridge Parkway for a

short trip into North Carolina. While in North Carolina we met Robin's stepdad, Donald Sherman, who drove up from South Carolina where he lived at the time.

Don Jim Robin

Photo by James Bruce

Don brought his fishing boat and we fished at a local lake near our next stop a unique location called Chimney Rock. Don, Rita, Robin, and I hiked the Chimney Rock Trail known as Skyline-Cliff Trail Loop which included sheer cliffs, breathtaking views, and the dramatic plunge of a waterfall. The Park was a real joy to be at but as we were climbing higher along the trail Robin realized the height she was at and froze while climbing a stairway. And I mean froze stiff with her hands it seemed attached to the railing. She was having a typical case of height fright. Her stepdad Don came to the rescue and coached her down the stairway after prying her hands off the railing. This two-hour, moderately strenuous hike coursed through lush woodland and across natural cliffs and ledges on its way to such geologic spectacles as the 2,280-foot-high top of the Chimney, the remarkable overhang and panoramic vistas at Opera Box, and the highest point in the park, 2,480-foot-tall Exclamation Point. Chimney Rock was an amazing sight! I would recommend it to everyone. After we dined and parted with Don, we headed for Grandfather Mountain the highest point of the Blue Ridge Mountains. I hiked to the top and I really enjoyed the view. Some things you cannot describe in words and the view, the excitement, and feelings of being on top of a mountain is one of them. For me it becomes a spiritual thing and I thank God for all the wonderful sights that I have seen.

From there we drove to Mt. Mitchell the highest point east of the Rockies. While driving to the top, I mentioned that we would be at the highest point. Both Robin and Rita would not even get out of the car. There are a few places in the world that still stand apart from the ordinary. Rising more than a mile high, surrounded by the gentle mist of low-hanging clouds, Mount Mitchell State Park is one of these extraordinary places. As we ascended this mighty peak, what looms in the horizon is a feast for the eyes—breathtaking views of the Blue Ridge Mountains, rolling ridges and fertile valleys. Forested and forever misty, 1,855-acre Mount Mitchell State Park will provide you with some of the most tranquil moments you will ever experience. That was as an exciting trip as I could have planned, but the next one was a trip of a lifetime because of the celebrity ELVIS PRESLEY.

As Robin, Rita and I drove to Elvis's mansion I was in shock at the location. I am sure when Elvis bought this home it was in the country back in 1956. Now it is in a part of the city that lets say needs some upgrading. Graceland was a bright spot in the community and to an Elvis fan like me, it was a thrill just to be there. It seemed the whole time we were there we could listen to sounds of Elvis which had me humming and singing along.

Photo by Wikipedia **Elvis Presley which I just found out is my 10th cousin on my mom's side of the family according to ancestry.com.**

Photos by James Bruce

We took every tour they offered which included Graceland, the Lisa Marie Airplane, the Elvis Tour Bus, and Elvis's grave site. For me to be at the home of the entertainer of my life who provided me with music, memories and movies was a dream come true. My only regret was that he was no longer with us.

Back at home my real estate business was slow, so I decided to look for another investor that wanted to invest in real estate property to rehab and resale and I found John Ruland a real estate manager for Saxton Real Estate Company. We found a property located at 1457 Lockbourne Road in Columbus that we bought and fixed up as planned. It was a 2 story 4-bedroom 2 bath single family house that a local Catholic Church owned. We made a deal with the church with little down and since it had no mortgage, we paid the church directly each month. John needed a place to live so while we fixed up the property he lived there, and he said he would make the payment to the church. Eventually, John would buy the house and I agreed to take it off the market.

1988 was a good year and our travels this year was closer to home with a trip to the best state park in the state of Ohio known as the Hocking Hills State Parks. Robin the kids and I really enjoyed the park with hikes throughout the Hocking Hills that were stunning. Located in the picturesque sandstone region of Southeastern Ohio, Hocking Hills State Park encompasses some of the most scenic areas in the entire state. Rock outcrops, deep cool gorges, and waterfalls are found throughout the 6 main park areas. The pristine beauty of the area is enhanced by the abundance of wildlife found throughout the Hocking region.

Our first stop was the most popular of all the Hocking Hills areas is Old Man's Cave, located on State Route 664. Here at the Upper Falls, the Grandma Gatewood Trail begins its six-mile course connecting three of the park's areas: Old Man's Cave to Cedar Falls to Ash Cave. This same trail has been designated as part of Ohio's Buckeye Trail as well as part of two national systems - the North Country Scenic Trail and America's Discovery Trail.

We then visited Ash Cave in the southernmost reaches of Hocking Hills, Ash Cave is beyond a doubt, the most spectacular feature of the entire park. Ash Cave is the largest, most impressive recess cave in the state.

Next, we stopped at Conkle's Hollow, situated off S.R. 374 on Big Pine Road. It is a rugged, rocky gorge and considered one of the deepest in Ohio. The valley floor is a veritable wilderness covered by a profusion of ferns and wildflowers with hemlock, birch, and other hardwood tower overhead. Our journey next took us to Cantwell Cliffs which is located in the northern reaches of Hocking Hills. It is 17 miles from Old Man's Cave on S.R. 374. Its remote location discourages visitation, but those who travel the extra distance will not be disappointed. Many visitors proclaim the Cantwell area as the most picturesque in Hocking County.

Going on was Cedar Falls, it is the greatest waterfall in terms of volume in the Hocking Hills region. Queer Creek tumbles over the face of the Blackhand displaying the awesome force of waterpower.

Old Man's Cave Upper Falls Ash Cave

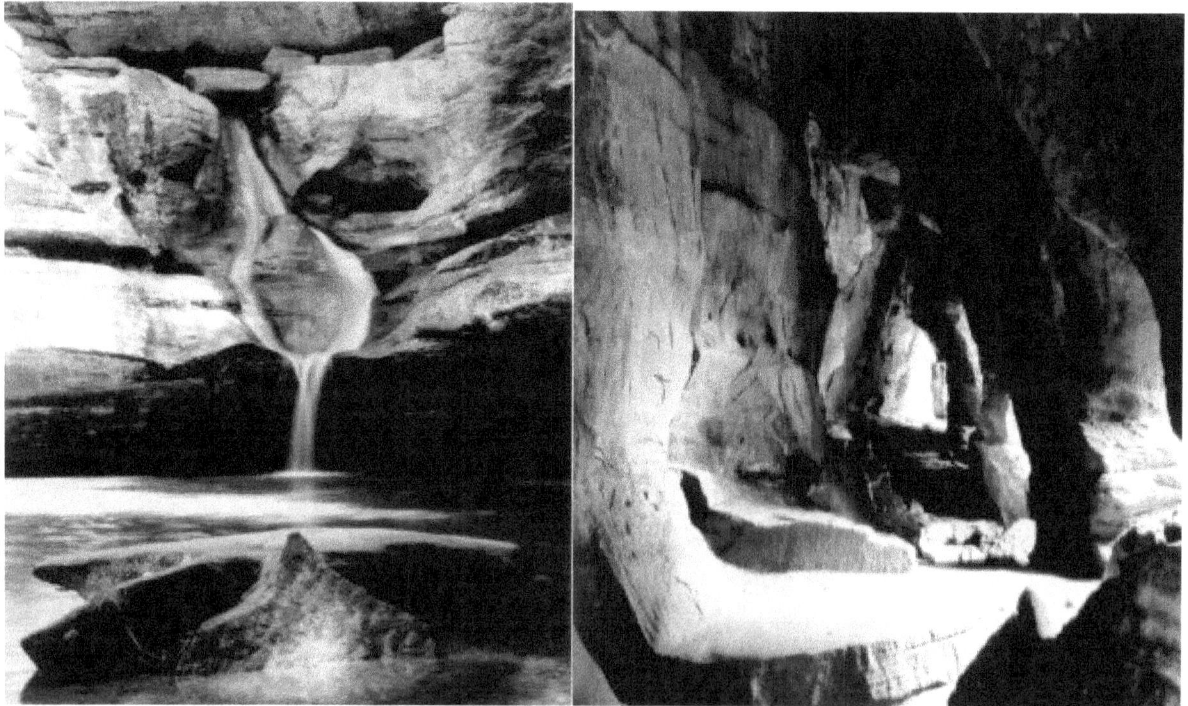

Cedar Falls Rock House

© Hocking Hills Studio Photography by Jason Campbell

Our last stop was Rock House State Park a unique place in the Hocking Hills' region, as it is the only true cave in the park. It is a tunnel-like corridor situated midway up a 150-foot cliff of Blackhand sandstone.

The second trip I took was a trip for the guys. I decided since I was doing so well, I would take (11) good friends that helped me in my career and a couple of old friends to a golf outing at Fairfield Glade Resorts.

Photo by James Bruce

I hosted and sponsored a golf tournament for two years known as the Jim Bruce Golf Tournament which consisted of 36 holes of golf on one of the best golf courses in the USA.

Photo by James Bruce

We stayed in a condo near the golf course, and everybody had a great time. I bought trophies for the winning teams and individual scorers. We had a blast, and everybody was incredibly grateful for the event. Since then, my good friends and golf buddies Pug Pepper and Ralph Montenaro have died.

I loved to play golf whenever I had the time. While playing golf with a few fellow real estate agents, a new friend by the name of Guy Devito, suggested we get together to flip some houses. Our plan was I would find the investments, evaluated the property, and then contract the property using my commission to close. Guy would then make and finance all the repairs and when the properties closed each of the investors would get their money back and we would share in the profits 50/50. I had found another investor in Guy, and we proceeded to buy up several properties at a time. You would think I would have learned the first time by not investing too much at one time. At the time I owned 3 other houses 2 single homes and 1 double of my own.

In 1988 my new partner Guy DeVito and I formed Team One Investments and bought 2 single family homes, 2 four family homes and 1 two family home. In May of 1989 we added another investor, Nancy Stone, and we bought 2 more 2 family homes. All these homes needed lots of repair, but we bought the homes for a decent price. The deal was the same as before any commission I earned as the Broker would be reinvested into the home plus

Nancy and Guy would invest in any additional monies needed to make the repairs. Guy would take care of all the subcontracting and oversee the repairs. At closing we would pay off all the debts and then split the profits.

Everything fell apart, the investors withdrew their money, the houses did not get repaired. I could not do anything with the properties, so I signed my share over to Guy. I just wanted to get out from under the problems realizing that I had made yet another mistake picking wrong partners. Nancy and I agreed to a settlement out of court.

In 1989 Nancy Stone recommended that I become the real estate broker for a new Real Estate Company owned by Dave Bible. The office would be located in Upper Arlington. I interviewed for the position as broker for Team First Real Estate and Dave hired me on the spot. On December 1, 1989, I decided to become a full-time insurance agent with an office in Grandview with Mike Snyder. On September 13th of 1990 John David Investments and I agreed that I would be their real estate broker for their new company Team First Real Estate located on Henderson Road in Upper Arlington. It consisted of 24 real estate agents. I closed my real estate office in West Jefferson.

Also, in 1989 Robin and I bought a ranch style house located at 4737 Midlane Drive Hilliard, Ohio consisting of 3 Bedrooms and 1 Bath on a large city lot for $58,000 from one of my agents. I put $10,000 down and financed $48,000. Chasity was 13 and Chad was 10 and although not as big as our previous house it was a nice house in a good community close to the schools. By this time, I had sold my other investments located at 1279 Indianola Ave. 109 Rodgers Ave., and the double on Scott Street in Columbus.

1989 was the year that I started Access Entertainment Group an entertainment bureau for musical talent and music. More about that later.

The music world from 1983 to 1989 brought us hits by Men at Work, Toto, Michael Jackson, David Bowie, Irene Cara, The Police, Billy Joel, Culture Club, Phil Collins, Yes, Van Halen, Deniece Williams, Cyndi Lauper, Duran Duran, Prince, Ray Parker Jr. Madonna, Foreigner, George Michael, Reo Speedwagon, Huey Lewis and the News, Dire Straits, Whitney Houston, Starship, Lionel Richie, Elton John, Heart, Robert Palmer, Billy Ocean, Genesis, Janet Jackson, Boston, Bon Jovi, U2, Tiffany, Gloria Estefan and the Miami Sound Machine, Guns and Roses, Def Leppard, Poison, Bette Midler, New Kids on the Block, and Paula Abdul.

Although I did not spend a lot of time watching television or even care to, television was transformed in the 1980s. With the advent of cable, the three major networks—ABC, CBS, and NBC, lost their monopoly on what Americans viewed in their living rooms. In the late Seventies, Time Inc.'s Home Box Office became available. In 1980, Ted Turner unveiled the Cable News Network (CNN), media baron Rupert Murdoch paid a billion dollars for Twentieth Century Fox, and, with Barry Diller, they created TV's fourth network, Fox.

In 1986, 82% of American adults watched television daily, and the average household had the television set on for seven hours a day. Sunday was the most popular night for television viewing, and the most popular form of television entertainment was the mini-series, followed by made-for-TV movies. Americans watched an average of 39 minutes of television news daily. By 1985, 68% of all American households (60 million) had cable television service, while 88% of those subscribed to a pay cable service like HBO or Showtime.

Cable was not the only culprit in ending the era of network television. Modern technologies resulted in the videocassette recorder, home video games and remote-control devices. According to *TV Guide*, "the remote-control switch revolutionized the way we watched TV in the 80s."

The decade was the golden age for primetime soap operas—*Dallas, Dynasty, Falcon Crest*, and *Knots Landing* all had their legions of faithful viewers. New life was breathed into the sitcom, with hit series like *The Cosby Show, Cheers, Family Ties* and the irreverent *Married. . .With Children.* The animated sitcom *The Simpsons* debuted in 1989, though Bart Simpson had previously made appearances on Fox's *The Tracey Ullman Show.* Top crime dramas like *Magnum P.I.* and *Hill Street Blues* enjoyed long runs in the 80s, while the innovative *Miami Vice* had a significant impact on television imagery. Programs like *thirtysomething* and *Moonlighting* appealed to the yuppie crowd. TV talk shows hosted by the likes of Geraldo Rivera and David Letterman became more provocative and occasionally outrageous.

The 1980s marked resurgence for Hollywood. The Eighties proved to be good years for Hollywood. The Eighties was the decade of the sequel, and in some cases the sequel was as good as (or even better than) and as commercially successful as the original. Harrison Ford's Indiana Jones became an American icon in *Raiders of the Lost Ark* (1981), *Indiana Jones and the Temple of Doom* (1984), and *Indiana Jones and the Last Crusade* (1989). Comic Eddie Murphy became a big star of the big screen with *Beverly Hills Cop* (1984) and *Beverly Hills Cop II* (1987). *Lethal Weapon* (1987) and *Die Hard* (1988) defined the action flick, and both spawned hit sequels. Sylvester Stallone's Rambo flexed America's muscles and represented the nation's renewed patriotic fervor in *First Blood* (1982), *Rambo: First Blood, Part II* (1985) and *Rambo III* (1988).

Some of my favorite movies during this decade included: Ghostbusters, Beverly Hills Cop, Indiana Jones, and the Temple of Doom, Grelims, The Karate Kid, Police Academy, Footloose, Romancing the Stone, Splash, Flashdance, Trading Places, War Games, Mr. Mom, Staying Alive, Risky Business, Top Gun, Crocodile Dundee, Platoon, Aliens, Ferris Bueller's Day Off, Fatal Attraction, The Untouchables, Lethal Weapon, Dirty Dancing, Rain Man, Big, and Die Hard.

The main events of the period included Heather Jean and Todd McDonald Tilton became parents of first set of twins conceived in vitro and born in the United States. Sally Ride becomes first American woman in space, Dr Barney Clark receives artificial heart implant, but dies 112 days after, Prime Minister Indira Gandhi was assassinated, the space shuttle Challenger explodes 74 seconds after lifting off, killing all seven crew members, including high school teacher Christa McAuliffe. The Soviet nuclear power plant located in Chernobyl had a partial meltdown releasing clouds of radiation across Europe. George Bush was elected as 41st U.S. President, Pan Am Flight 103 explodes, The Exxon Valdez oil spill making it the largest oil spill in US history and the fall of the Berlin Wall.

The 1990's was a time of gradual improvement and lots of changes for the Bruce household. We had settled into our house in Hilliard. Chasity was now 14 and Chad was 11 were entrenched in the local school system. Robin was a cosmetologist at a local salon, and I was terribly busy, as usual, selling real estate, insurance, and starting a business as entertainment manager for local entertainers. The first entertainer that I managed was a 19-year-old male country singer by the name of John Crabtree. My good friend of mine John Notter, make that Rev John Notter whom I met at Elston Richards Storage in 1970 asked me if I would like to be an auctioneer and help him with a few sales. I thought that would be a promising idea and said yes. So, I went to the state licensing bureau and tested and passed to become an apprentice auctioneer. I helped John with a few sales and after a year I decided that I did not have time or interest to continue so I cancelled my license to auction.

Photos by James Bruce

At the home front Chasity was now a teenager and completely boy crazy. She was a lot for her mother to handle so occasionally I had to step in to protect Chasity from her mom. Chasity's first year at high school was one that found her grounded almost the entire year. Chad was struggling to keep his head about water at school but to his credit he worked at keeping out of trouble. Both kids were great children with a good attitude and Robin, and I thoroughly enjoyed our lives with them. Matter of fact whenever the kids were not with us, we missed them and the fun they brought us. I rarely got mad, and I always tried to treat the kids fairly. But when I got mad, they did not forget it and I made it a point to let them not forget it. One-time Chad called his mom a nasty word and it was time for an attitude adjustment so I went into his room and literally kicked and tossed him from his room to the living room so he could apologize to his mom. He did and Chad still remembers that little episode of discipline as one he will never forget as a lesson learned.

By August 1992 Team First was becoming a successful Real Estate office with sales exceeding 14 million dollars and the owners decided to sell Team First Real Estate. On February 16, 1993, they merged with King Thompson Real Estate. I decided to return as my own brokerage of Bruce Real Estate along with 4 agents and relocated my Real Estate business to my Grandview Office. 1992 was the year that I signed my second entertainer to my record label originally called J. Paul Records. Her name was Debbie Collins a female country singer.

In 1992 John Notter and I decided to invest in a couple of properties and purchased a tax foreclosure located at 1613 Elmore and rehabber located at 2487 Osceola Ave. in Columbus. We sold both properties for a profit with a short turn around especially the Elmore property which we sold in just 1 week. My real estate purchases proved successful at last.

A sad time for our family was the passing of my dad from a stroke while mom and dad were living in Arizona. He was 71 years old. He was a great dad who I miss a lot and one of hardest working people that anyone ever met. Dad was a splendid example for all his 7 kids. Being the oldest child, I really enjoyed being with him whenever I could.

In 1994 Chasity graduated from Hilliard High School as a Junior. Chad was now 15 years old decided to move to Marion, Ohio where his father lived and to be closer to his friends. My mom died while living at my sister Linda's house in Springfield, Ohio. She died of heart failure at the age of 67. Mom, the mother of 7 children spent most of her younger life, of course, being mom to all of us. Before the children started to arrive, she worked and then again after we the children grew up, she went back to work. She was smart and had a great personality. Mom kept us in line when dad was not home. We all loved Mom.

Photo by James Bruce

The year was 1994 and I signed my third entertainer Brandi Lynn Howard a 10-year-old female country singer, to a recording contract. I also renamed my record label to Spotlight Records.

IN JANUARY 1994 CHASITY married Jeremy Vance and in May of that same year they celebrated the birth of Courtney Vance, our first granddaughter.

Courtney

Photo by James Bruce

In 1995 is the year we sold the house on Midlane Drive in Hilliard for $80,000 and we moved to an apartment located in Hilliard to pay off some debt that had mounted up through my investment in the music business.

It was the year 1996 while I was working my real estate and insurance business, that I was approached by a client of mine and asked if I would be interested in becoming an assistant manager of hers at the largest newspaper in Ohio called the Columbus Dispatch. At the time, I needed more money to continue in the entertainment business which at that time I was promoting Debbie Collins and her new CD worldwide. I worked for the Dispatch on the weekends it was about the only time I could be available. I did that for 2 years then became a District Manager full time for 2 more years. I have continued to work for the Columbus Dispatch part time as an Independent Contractor ever since then.

In 1997 our 2nd grandchild Jacob Paul (named after me, same middle names) was born to Chasity and Jeremy Vance. I was present at the request of my daughter to the live birth. This was a new experience and something I will never forget. A baby entering this world from his mother's womb and witnessing his first breath. WOW!

In the year 2000 at the age of 54, I decided to retire from real estate and insurance after 24 years in real estate and 18 years in the insurance business. I guess I wanted to concentrate on my entertainment business and newspaper distribution. This was also the year that I met or was introduced to our daughter's mother-in-law, Vicki Vance.

In 2001 Robin and I decided to travel again, and we were excited about returning to Colorado to see my brother Cliff. Of course, we would see some new sites along the way. Our first stop was to visit the Indianapolis Speedway where we took a guided bus tour around the racetrack. We then stopped at the raceway museum to take in all cars past and future and more history of the track.

Harry Miller Display in Hall of Fame.

Photos by James Bruce

We left Indianapolis Indiana heading southwest to our next stop, Saint Louis Missouri, there we had the thrill of taking a gondola to the top of the St Louis Archway to experience a unique view of St. Louis and the surrounding areas. Also, while we were there, we spent some time at the museum and enjoyed the parkway. Our next stop was a visit to the very educational George Washington Carver birthplace memorial and museum. While in Colorado we made it a point to stop at the Great Sand Dunes National Monument and of course we spent 3 days with my brother, Cliff.

Picture by James Bruce

The Music Business

Photo by James Bruce

In 1989 at the age of 43 I decided to make a career move for the future and the total enjoyment of something that I felt God introduced me to. I began this business in July of 1989 as a talent agent and manager. My first performer was a lead singer for a band that was called Country Comfort. The drummer's daughter, a friend of my daughter, mentioned they were looking for a place to practice. My daughter Chasity suggested to the band that they practice in a finished part of a small barn on our property in West Jefferson, Ohio. Robin and I agreed that it would be ok. After a few practices, my wife, Robin encouraged that I stop to listen to this singer and his band one evening after work. After I listened to the band one night, I suggested that they get a manager to help their career. The band agreed and asked me if I would be interested in helping them. I knew nothing about managing a band, but it sounded exciting so I thought I would give it a try. The lead singers name was John Crabtree.

Photo by James Bruce

John and his band pictured above. The band was ok for a local band but the lead singer, as Robin had suggested was good. I suggested after promoting them for about a year that I should manage John. I felt that he was that good. John and his wife had just got married not too long before he started practicing with the band and he already had one child with another one on the way at the time. I decided to take John to Nashville where he got a chance to sing on Music Row where he attracted a good crowd that appreciated his talents. I then entered him into a talent contest at the legendary Broken Spoke. John placed 4th out of 19 performers, and he was the only one not from Nashville. I told John he was a complete package with "looks, stage presence and vocals" and he had a great future in the music industry if he would persist. I booked John and his band until May 1992 when the band disbanded, and John decided to leave the entertainment industry to support his family. Pictures provided by James Bruce.

After John's band split up one of the guitar players, James Lancia; mentioned to my wife he was playing in a band called Pryme Tyme and Debbie Collins. She went to watch them, and she came back with a story that I had to go see this group and its lead singer. She was fantastic!!! In August of 1992 I signed Debbie Collins to a personal and business management agreement.

Debbie and I signing our contract with BMI

Picture by James Bruce

Because of Debbie's songwriting ability it was determined that we needed a publishing company to publish her songs. In 1994 we established James Paul Music, a publishing company through BMI. To promote Debbie's music and advance her career it was obvious we needed to record Debbie and release her first CD. After further consideration I decided to take Debbie to Nashville and record her debut album in 1995. For 7 or 8 months before that I listened to several hundred songs that I considered for her album and every time I found a song that might work, I sent it to Debbie to get her opinion. Debbie and I finally agreed on 10 songs most of them written by legendary songwriters.

Debbie Collins in Hilltop Studios Nashville, Tennessee produced and engineered by John Nicholson and Mike "Chickenhawk." Also pictured the studio musicians charting the songs.

The songwriters on the Cd included 1) Buddy Brock, who co-wrote Watermelon Crawl for Tracy Byrd and also wrote hit songs for Tim McGraw, Aaron Tippin, Alan Jackson, and Kenny Chesney. 2) Bob McDill, wrote songs for artists such as Jerry Lee Lewis[1], Anne Murray[2], Don Williams[3], Waylon Jennings[4], Keith Whitley, Crystal Gayle, Bobby Bare, Juice Newton, the Kendalls, Alan Jackson, Mel McDaniels, Pam Tillis, Doug Stone and Mickey Gilley[5]. 3) Donny Kees, who wrote hits for Bryan White, Daryl Singletary, Kevin Sharp, Ricochet, and co-wrote the song "Brokenheartsville" for Joe Nichols and he also co-wrote the song "I Believe" for the group Diamond Rio. 4) Kostas Lazarides, wrote for Patty Loveless[6], Dwight Yoakam, McBride & the Ride[7], Travis Tritt[8], Holly Dunn[9], Martina McBride[10], The Mavericks[11]. and singer songwriter Marty Stewart.

---

1. https://en.wikipedia.org/wiki/Jerry_Lee_Lewis

2. https://en.wikipedia.org/wiki/Anne_Murray

3. https://en.wikipedia.org/wiki/Don_Williams

4. https://en.wikipedia.org/wiki/Waylon_Jennings

5. https://en.wikipedia.org/wiki/Mickey_Gilley

6. https://en.wikipedia.org/wiki/Patty_Loveless

7. https://en.wikipedia.org/wiki/McBride_%26_the_Ride

8. https://en.wikipedia.org/wiki/Travis_Tritt

The CD was titled "That's the Way" and received lots of heavy airplay, especially in Europe. Acquiring booking agents for this exceptionally beautiful and talented artist became a priority and before long I had her and her new band "Wildride" booked on the Carnival Cruise Line thanks to Marty Martel of Midnight Productions of Nashville, Tennessee. Next, I arranged for The Good Music Agency of Las Vegas and St. Paul Minnesota to book Debbie and Wildride from then on. The Good Music Agency booked Debbie for the next 4 years. After 4 years on the road Debbie met, her current husband, married and settled down in Minnesota.

Debbie charted at #74 and I ended up spending a total of $93,000 not counting my time valued at $52,000 a year for 2 years and $36,000 a year for 5 years on Debbie's project for a total of 7 years.

---

9. https://en.wikipedia.org/wiki/Holly_Dunn

10. https://en.wikipedia.org/wiki/Martina_McBride

11. https://en.wikipedia.org/wiki/The_Mavericks

Radio Biella   FAX 0039-15-352448   BIELLA   ITALY

WOODPECKER *country, bluegrass, old time and folk music*

D.J. PELLA ALFONSO & TABACCHINI GINO   VIA REGIONE SETTERIO 35 CHIAVAZZA 13051 BIELLA   ITALY

PLAYLIST   date 28 MARCH 1996 / 31 MARCH 1996   radio program n° 225

SONG TITLE	ARTIST	ALBUM	LABEL
THIS CAN'T BE ANYTHING But LOVE	DEBBIE COLLINS	THAT'S THE WAY	J. PAUL REC.
CALLIN' YOUR NAME	RICKY SKAGGS	SOLID GROUND	ATLANTIC
DADDY'S MONEY	RICOCHET	RICOCHET	COLUMBIA
BLOWIN' SMOKE	DAVID BALL	THINKIN PROBLEM	WB
LIVIN ALONE TOGHETER	CHRISTOPHER LEE CLAYTON		COMSTOCK
MY WHOLE WIDE WORLD	RADNEY FOSTER	LABOR OF LOVE	ARISTA
READ BETWEEN THE LINES	AARON TIPPIN	READ BETWEEN THE LINES	BMG
DON'T LOOK NOW	ARCHER & PARK	WE GOT A LOT IN COMMON	ATLANTIC
IT'S ALL A SHOW	BETHANY REYNOLDS	SHOOTING STAR	AARROW
AIN'T NO GETTIN WELL	NORWOOD CARTER	LONESOME MEMORIES	MESQUITE
WHEREVER SHE IS	RICKY VAN SHELTON	LOVE AND HONOR	COLUMBIA
STONES IN THE ROAD	MARY CHAPIN CARPENTER	STONES IN THE ROAD	COLUMBIA
AIN'T NO TRAIN	IANN BROWNE	TELL ME WHY	CURB
ANYWAY YOU WANA MY LOVE	DETOUR	HONKY TONKIN' TIL IT HURTS	LASERLIGHT
JUST BETWEEN THE TWO OF US	DEBBIE COLLINS	THAT'S THE WAY	J. PAUL REC.
I WANT TO FEEL THE PAIN	JIMMY TITTLE	IT'S IN THE ATTITUDE	DIXIE FROG
OLD HEART	INGER NORDSTRÖM	LIVING WITH A BROKEN HEART	
GOOD NEWS FROM HOME	BEPPE GAMBETTA	GOOD NEWS FROM HOME	GREEN LINNETT
HE HAD A LONG CHAIN ON	TIM O'BRIEN	OH BOY! O'BOY!	SUGAR HILL
SITTIN' ON GO	BRYAN WHITE	BETWEEN NOW AND FOREVER	ASYLUM
C.O.U.N.T.R.Y.	JOE DIFFIE	LIFE'S SO FUNNY	EPIC
SHE NEVER LOOKS BACK	DOUG SUPERNAW	YOU STILL GOT ME	GIANT
ALL I WANT IS A LIFE	TIM McGRAW	NOT A MOMENT TOO SOON	CURB
GOD'S COUNTRY USA	MARCUS HUMMON	ALL IN GOOD TIME	COLUMBIA

Just one of many playlists I received from Europe. Check out the competition!! Debbie was a big hit especially in Germany where she and George Jones fought it out for most played country songs in 1996.

Debbie and her band Pryme Tyme Debbie and her band that went on the cruise

Photos by James Bruce

Photos by James Bruce

Debbie Collins debut CD with J Paul Records later changed to Spotlight Records

While I got Debbie on the road in 1994, I started looking for a new preferably young male artist to promote. Not!!! I spotted Brandi Lynn Howard at an American Legion Post in Hilliard, Ohio while attending an Ohio Country Western Music Association meeting. I was so impressed with this young female talent (only 10 years old) I knew right then that this young performer and vocalist had what it takes to be a success in the entertainment industry. Within 2 months I signed Brandi to a management contract. Brandi went on to perform in Las Vegas,

Nevada; Nashville, Tennessee and throughout the Midwest at fairs, festivals, concerts, and conventions which I booked.

Brandi and I at my office where I explained to her the terms of the contract agreed to by Brandi, her mom and grandmother.

Photo by James Bruce

Photos by James Bruce

Pictured above is Brandi and her band that travelled to Las Vegas where they won 2 awards, the same award that Leann Rimes won a few years before. Later, Brandi and I created a record label known as "Spotlight Records" to promote her music. In 1999-2000 we completed Brandi's first CD "Only in a Picture" which has received airplay all over the world. Brandi helped produce, wrote, and co-wrote this successful first effort at the age of 16.

Photo provided by Lary Lee Photography

Brandi has been on numerous TV shows and featured as far away as Japan on NHK-TV Worldwide Release. She also has won so many music awards that she has a small museum in her basement to display her many accomplishments. Dark blonde hair and brown eyes, along with a beautiful smile make Brandi's appearance like that of a princess. Her petite frame belied the powerful range of her vocal talent, proving the adage "big things come in small packages". Brandi had the musical background and experience of someone many years older. In 2002 Brandi was hired by the Longaberger Basket Company as an Entertainer for one of the largest companies in Ohio. Brandi was my first artist that went big on the internet.

At that time, I had her on over 100 music websites, and she charted on one site at that time called mp3.com. I ended spending a little over $67,000 not counting my time which has been valued at $26,000 a year on Brandi for 7 years. I booked her at gigs all over the Midwestern part of the country from 1994 till 2000.

Photo by Lary Lee Photography

Brandi Lynn Howard at the age of 16

While Debbie was on tour, I had the pleasure of attending a concert by Sara Evans by special invitation from Mark Schelske keyboard player for Sara. Mark also played the keyboard for Brandi Lynn Howard when available making the trip to Ohio on available weekends. (Pictured below)

Photo by James Bruce

Photo by https://en.wikipedia.org/wiki/Sara_Evans

Sara Lynn Evans is an American country music singer and songwriter. Evans has also won one award each from Billboard, the Academy of Country Music, the Country Music Association, Broadcast Music Incorporated, and a Dove Award.

In the year 2002 I decided that it was time for me to cut back so I decided to be a consultant after 14 years as a music publishing, music promoter, merchandiser, webmaster, record, video and TV producer, talent manager, talent agent, and record label owner. My new company was called Access Talent and for more than two years I consulted with and advised singers, songwriters, and bands on how to go about their careers. That was fun, but I admit I did miss the excitement of the real music business. In 2004 I was approached by a bass player by the name of Jon Hawks of the band known as Category IV in the hopes they might become a client.

Category IV

signing their contract

Photos by James Bruce

HERE ARE JON'S THOUGHTS on what happened "For those of you who don't know, and I am aware that most of you do, but for those who don't, here is the story behind our recording contract. I (Jon) had been running the "behind the scenes" stuff for the band and felt we were ready for the next step. I sent out several promotional packages to agents and management companies about the band. I received a few responses but the one who seemed most interested was Jim Bruce of Access Talent. Jim came to just ONE of our shows at the Dugout and was "hit by the storm" that IS Category IV. Jim began giving me advice, pulling from his experience with several musical acts and I listened. Jim then offered to manage the band. Jay, Donnie, Mike, and I all discussed it and went to a meeting at Jim's house. All agreed to move forward with Access Talent and Jim as our manager. Come to find out. Jim owned a record label by the name of Spotlight Records. Again, several meetings, some tweaking' of the contract and BOOM, we were signed at a big party held at Dough Boys in Ashville early in 2005!"

Jim in his office Galloway

Photo by James Bruce

PHOTOS BY JAMES BRUCE

So, in 2005 I decided that I would like to produce my third CD titled "The Storm" by Category IV. The process of finding a studio that fit all the criteria the band and what I was looking for took a few months. I contacted studios in Washington D.C., Virginia, Ohio, Indiana, Tennessee, and New York. We settled on a studio in New York. This place was just blocks from Central Park, in the heart of Manhattan. This guy has done work with artist like James Taylor and Madonna. We were going up to do just 3 or 4 songs and release those while we

Photo by Lary Lee Photography

worked on the rest of the CD. Then, I discovered a studio in Lafayette, Indiana by the name of Sound Logic. Sound Logic has earned several awards including 2 Grammy nominations generated from work in this studio. Time for a "road trip." The band and I all packed into Mikes (the drummer) van and off we went. We misjudged the time it would take us but a Ponderosa dinner and 5 hours later, we arrived at the Sound Logic studio. You would never know it was a studio. Out in the middle of nowhere, you would just see this nice house with a pole barn next to it and assume nothing! Go into the pole barn and you are in a whole different world. Finished and equipped with recording gear, a grand piano, separate rooms for vocal recording and a HUGE control room overlooking the main studio. Two hours later and we were no longer going to New York. The owner of Sound Logic, Jeff Anderson, made me an offer I could not refuse. Jeff was born in 1976 and has accomplished a great deal throughout his varied career. Jeff began his career working in the music industry as a musician. While recording in the studio, he found true enjoyment in the art of recording music. Following this newfound interest, he attended the prestigious Full Sail School of Recording Arts and began work as a sound engineer. In 1996, Jeff founded and built Sound Logic Recording Studios in Saint Joseph, Missouri. Over the next 5 years, Jeff produced over 480 productions that received national syndication and built the studio into one of the 100 largest recording studios in the US. Jeff's work at Sound Logic, has earned him many national and international awards including Grammy® nominations, Addy Awards, Communicator Awards, Telly Awards, Aegis Awards, and an International Cindy Award. He has worked in all levels of the music, advertising, and film industries. In 2004 Jeff moved to Lafayette IN and achieved his dream, "a world class recording facility in a laid-back secluded location." Category IV recorded at Jeff Anderson's private 1600 sq foot studio. Sound Logic houses a vintage Neve 8108 console. One of 6 left in the USA. This console has recorded over 30 number one hits in the past and has a unique warm feel about it. I released this CD to radio in 2007. I ended spending $34,000 not counting my time which has been valued at $52,000 a year over a 2-year period on Category IV. The band disbanded shortly after that.

———————————

TODD BERRY AND JIM Bruce signing his contract

Photos by James Bruce **Jim in Studio**

2008 brought me a unique talent in Todd Berry, a rock and country act from Muncie, Indiana. Mr. Berry contacted my wife and after many attempts trying to reach me without success my wife suggested that I contact that kid from Indiana telling me he was very persistent. I invited Todd to come to my home to audition for us. He gladly accepted and auditioned for us on our back patio singing with music tracks. He really impressed me and on August 25, 2008, Spotlight Records signed Todd Berry to a recording contract. I finished recording Todd Berry's 4 song EP titled Better Days to Cry early in 2009 and released the EP in March of 2009. We followed that up with a full Cd of the same title. Late in the 2009 I got Todd signed to Tate Music of Tate Publishing out of Mustang, Oklahoma to a recording contract. That Cd titled There He Is was released in 2010. Todd born legally blind, but not once has it held him back from the first and the last thing on his mind, music. Todd has been singing since the age of nine, had successfully made a living doing what he loves – singing and performing since the age of 15. Todd has been influenced by several artists including Elvis Presley, Garth Brooks, Huey Lewis, Lynard Skynard and more. Todd also writes and produces original music of his and other artists. Todd Berry is a professional singer that has provided entertainment for clubs and venues throughout the United States, Todd performs a wide variety of music ranging from 50s & 60s Classic Rock, Country, and Gospel music.

Latest release March 22, 2021, Todd as Elvis

Photos provided by Todd Berry

The International Association of Independent Recording Artists, IAIRA[12], recognizes and honors artistic achievement, technical proficiency, and overall excellence in sound recording by monitoring chart activity as published in various reporting charts from around the world. According to their research, on 07/30/2010 the above referenced release; Politically Incorrect Redneck, a song on the CD by Todd Berry, had attained The Number 52 Position on at least one of the charts monitored and verified by IAIRA[13]. Based on that research,

---

12. http://www.iaira.com/

13. http://www.iaira.com/

IAIRA[14] has qualified the release as eligible for Certification as an International 'Top 100'. I resigned Todd Berry to a new recording contract in 2020. I ended up spending over $36,000 dollars not counting my time which has been valued at $52,000 a year on Todd's project for a total of 4 years. Todd paid me back over $10,000 dollars which I reinvested on the Todd Berry Project.

In 2016 I signed Kalysta Minton, a 14-year-old female country singer, to a recording contract thanks to an agent and friend of mine that I have known since jr. high school Darrel Riggs.

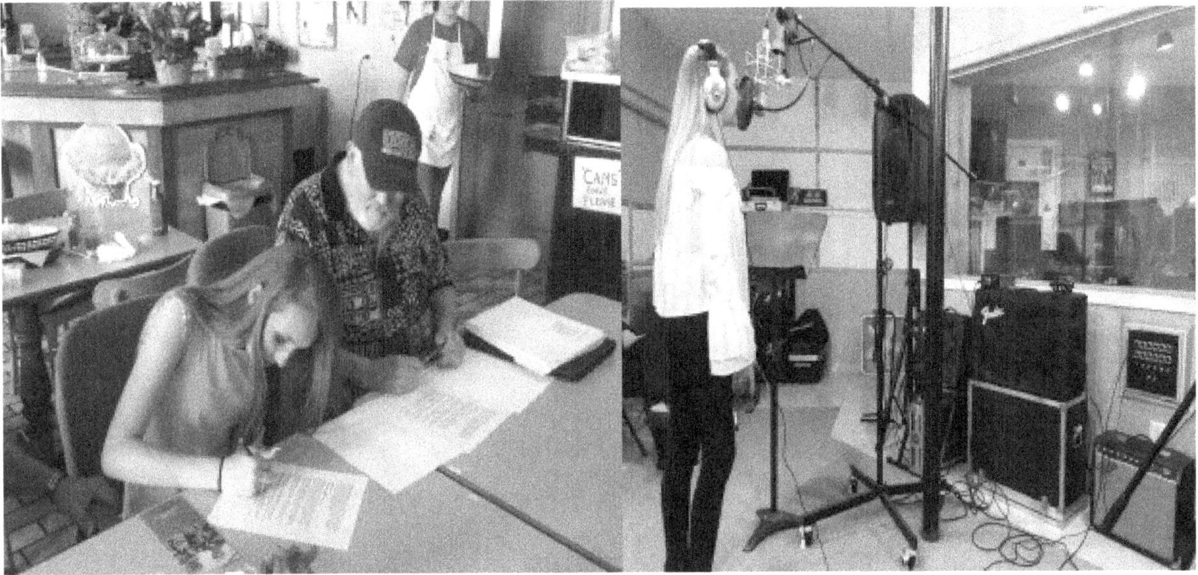

Signing Kalysta at the age of 14 Kalysta in the studio at the age of 17

Kalysta, John Pineiro, musician and Jim Kalysta, Jim, and Glenn Minton (Dad)

Photos by James Bruce

14. http://www.iaira.com/

Photos by ProDuctions/Pam Egbert

Kalysta Minton

Her voice has been described at times as angelic and magical. Darrel Riggs agent for Access Entertainment Group said "I like her mostly because of her amazing, distinguishable and remarkable vocals. Her choice of song is

extraordinary and whenever I listen to her sing, it gives me chills." Photo by James Bruce

Darrel and Jim 60 years later who met in Jr. High School.

Darrel Riggs, agent for Access Entertainment Group, discovered Kalysta at a Winterfest and suggested to me "that we consider her talent for future projects, she is an unbelievable talent for her age." At that time, Kalysta was managed and booked by Mr. Chris Branham once the leader of the Dick Clark Band back in the 1970's. After several meetings with Kalysta's parents, Kim, and Glenn Minton, all have agreed that this contract is in the best interest for her music career.

Photo by **Darrel Riggs**   Photo by **Chris Branham**

Photo by James Bruce

Glenn, Kim (Mom), Jim and Kalysta celebrating her EP release

Kalysta has had the privilege of performing at the Clinton County Fair, Brown County Fair, Clermont County Fair, The Famous Murphy Theater and has appeared on Channel 4 News in Nashville Tennessee! Kalysta has also performed at the famous Horse Drawn Carriage Parade in Lebanon, Ohio, the Rising Star Casino in Rising Sun, Indiana, and at the famous Tootsies Lounge in Nashville just to mention a few. Other accomplishments include a performance at Cincinnati's Famous Dinner Club, Jim n Jacks on The River and entertained at the Community Arts Theatre, Fairfield, Ohio for their 60th Anniversary of the City! The mayor just loved her!! She is currently working on her debut CD in Nashville. This year 2021, we expect now that the COVID number of infections has improved that Kalysta and Todd Berry's gigs will pick up and scheduling will resume. Let us pray.

In 2017 I signed David Church to my label a traditional male country TV star that was featured on RFD-TV for over 15 years. David's first CD with Spotlight Records titled "Keepin Tradition" was released in 2018. David Church is recognized for his authentic rendition of "Hank Williams". And he is recognized by music historians, celebrities, and family members as the "#1 tribute to Hank". The RFDTV network has grown rapidly and is now broadcast to over 65 million viewers throughout the US. David has been featured as a regular on the popular show "Midwest Country". It is easy to understand why he is RFD-TV's "most requested" artist. Amazingly, without a major hit on mainstream radio, Church has millions of fans all over the world. David performs throughout the

world along with his talented wife, Terri Lisa Church. Terri Lisa is also a recording artist/songwriter. She sings lead and backup vocals. Terri Lisa is a published journalist. David and Lisa are continuing doing what the love to do and that is entertaining.

Photos by David and Terri Lisa Church

Photo by James Bruce

Here Jim is with Pam Egbert on the right with the cast of Bob Braun Show Rob Reider, Nancy James, and our good friend Mark Preston.

I have met, worked with, and booked many artists over the years. My first big name that I met was Kenny Rogers at an independent music one on one convention in Nashville, Tennessee.

Kenny Rogers

Photos and info provided by https://en.wikipedia.org/wiki/Kenny_Rogers

(August 21, 1938 – March 20, 2020) was an American singer, songwriter, musician, actor, record producer, and entrepreneur. He was elected to the Country Music Hall of Fame[15] in 2013. Rogers was particularly popular with country audiences but also charted more than 120 hit singles across various music genres, topping the country and pop album charts for more than 200 individual weeks in the United States alone. He sold more than 100 million records worldwide during his lifetime, making him one of the best-selling music artists of all time[16]. His fame and career spanned multiple genres: jazz, folk, pop, rock, and country. He remade his career and was one of the most successful cross-over artists of all time.

Here are more artists that I have worked with including Richard Marx thanks to agent Pam Egbert pictured below.

---

15. https://en.wikipedia.org/wiki/Country_Music_Hall_of_Fame_and_Museum

16. https://en.wikipedia.org/wiki/List_of_best-selling_music_artists

Pam Egbert by Pam Egbert Richard Marx Photo Poster created by James Bruce

Info provided by Richard Marx - Wikipedia[17]

Richard Marx (born September 16, 1963) is a Grammy[18]-winning American adult contemporary[19] and pop/rock[20] singer, songwriter, musician, and record producer.

Marx's self-titled debut album went triple-platinum in 1987, and his first single, "Don't Mean Nothing[21]", reached number three in the charts. Between 1987 and 1994, he had 14 Top 20 hits, including three number one singles; his first seven singles all reached the Top Five. His singles during the late 1980s and 1990s included "Endless Summer Nights[22]", "Hold On to the Nights[23]", "Right Here Waiting[24]", "Now and Forever[25]", "Hazard[26]", and "At the Beginning[27]" with Donna Lewis[28].

Jim and Richard Marx Backstage / Photos by James Bruce

Thanks to agent Annette Clarke with Jim Bruce

17. https://en.wikipedia.org/wiki/Richard_Marx

18. https://en.wikipedia.org/wiki/Grammy

19. https://en.wikipedia.org/wiki/Adult_contemporary_music

20. https://en.wikipedia.org/wiki/Pop_rock

21. https://en.wikipedia.org/wiki/Don%E2%80%99t_Mean_Nothing

22. https://en.wikipedia.org/wiki/Endless_Summer_Nights

23. https://en.wikipedia.org/wiki/Hold_On_to_the_Nights

24. https://en.wikipedia.org/wiki/Right_Here_Waiting

25. https://en.wikipedia.org/wiki/Now_and_Forever_(Richard_Marx_song)

26. https://en.wikipedia.org/wiki/Hazard_(song)

27. https://en.wikipedia.org/wiki/At_the_Beginning

28. https://en.wikipedia.org/wiki/Donna_Lewis

Photo by James Bruce

We booked Confederate Railroad

Confederate Railroad

Photo provided by Access Entertainment Group of Indiana

Thanks to agent George Kidder we arranged for Tanya Tucker to appear at the Seacrest Auditorium and Music Hall, and we signed a marketing agreement to market her show.

Photo by James Bruce

Jim and George Kidder best friends and associates. George was my Senior Vice President for a few years and later started his own company. We also booked local, regional, and National acts such as:

Photo provided by **Stadium 11**

Photo provided by Brad Puckett

Brad Puckett

Photo provided by The Professors

Photo by The Conspiracy Band

The Conspiracy Band

and Tanya Tucker

Photo   and   info   provided   by   Tanya   Tucker

Tanya Denise Tucker (born October 10, 1958) is an American country music singer and songwriter who had her first hit, "Delta Dawn[29]", in 1972 at the age of 13. Over the succeeding decades, Tucker became one of the few child performers to mature into adulthood without losing her audience, and during the course of her career, she notched a streak of top-10 and top-40 hits.

---

29. https://en.wikipedia.org/wiki/Delta_Dawn

Photo by Larry Alessio

Good friend and musician agent Larry Alessio. Great Drummer for several of my acts. Later Larry started his own agency.

Photo by Mila Mason

Mila Mason whom we met in her office in Nashville. Mila Mason (born August 22, 1963) is an American country music artist. She made her debut on the country music scene in 1996 with the release of her debut album That's Enough of That, which produced three hit singles on the Billboard.

Larry Jim and George

Photo by James Bruce

Other acts we worked with included Baillie and the Boys who Brandi opened up for at the Palace Theatre in Marion, Ohio. Kimberly Caldwell's (pictured below) mom contacted me while Debbie Collins was at a convention showcasing. She asked me if I would manage her daughter hearing I was a successful agent. Unfortunately, I was too busy to manage anyone else. Kimberly Ann Caldwell (born February 25, 1982) is an American singer[30], actress[31] and television hostess[32], from Katy, Texas[33]. She rose to fame when she was a finalist on the second season[34] of *American Idol*[35]. After her American Idol stint, Caldwell was an entertainment correspondent and hosted various shows on the TV Guide Network[36]. She released her debut album *Without Regret*[37] on April 19, 2011. Sign to Capital Records.

Robin and I met Donna Fargo at what is now called the CMA Fest where I showcased both Debbie Collins and Brandi Lynn Howard early in the 1990s thanks to IFCO and the Johnson Sisters who started Loretta Lynn's fan club.

---

30. https://en.wikipedia.org/wiki/Singing

31. https://en.wikipedia.org/wiki/Actor

32. https://en.wikipedia.org/wiki/Television_presenter

33. https://en.wikipedia.org/wiki/Katy,_Texas

34. https://en.wikipedia.org/wiki/American_Idol_(season_2)

35. *https://en.wikipedia.org/wiki/American_Idol*

36. https://en.wikipedia.org/wiki/TV_Guide_Network

37. *https://en.wikipedia.org/wiki/Without_Regret*

George booked Tommy Cash and the Cash Crew for a corporate party in Newark, Ohio

Photos by James Bruce

Jim and Jesse McReynolds Bluegrass Hall of Fame members and stars of the Grand Ole Opry are cousins of mine on my mom's side.

Life Continues

Chasity marriage to Jeremy Vance failed and she remarried to Joseph Caldwell in 2007 who had 3 children from a previous marriage. We added those children Joey, Isaiah, and Trinity to our family.

Chasity and Joe at their wedding

Photo by Chasity Caldwell

In the year 2010 I was super busy as usual with the Dispatch and the entertainment business that my health became a concern. I noticed my breathing was becoming labored more every day. Finally, on the 9th of December while delivering magazines to a movie theatre in downtown Columbus I was climbing the stairs to the entrance when I had to stop and rest on a step. I did not feel good and decided to quit what I was doing and drive home to rest. It was later that night early in the morning of the 10th I went to the kitchen window. I was feeling very weak, and my heart was pounding, I opened the window up for some fresh air. I knew I was in trouble. I drove myself to the nearest hospital. I was 64 years old.

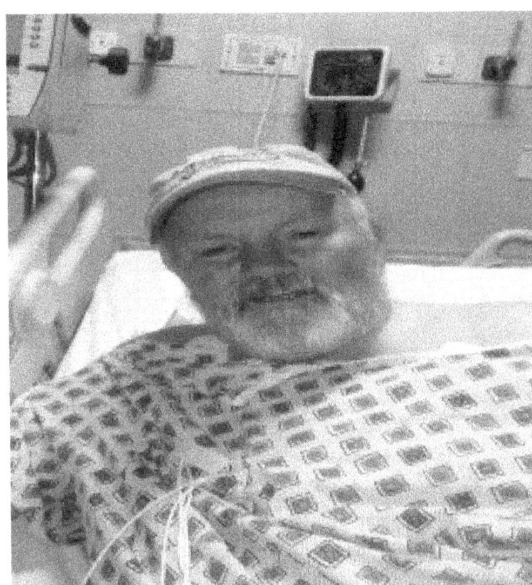

Jim in hospital

Photo by James Bruce

I was admitted immediately and was informed I was having a heart attack and the nurses and doctors needed to run tests on me to see how much damage there was. Thank God, I only needed 2 stints in one vein which had 70% blockage. The doctor on duty who operated on me said everything came out fine and wished me well. But by June 2011 the stints were not working as well and after a stress test performed at the VA clinic it was determined that I needed 3 more stents, those were to go inside the older ones. The first stents were a bit older, and these new ones would work better. They have since then.

2011 found my marriage to Robin had become strained at best and she filed for divorce which was final in 2012. So, after 29 years together it was time to call it quits. For most of those 29 years our marriage was the greatest. I loved her more than anything in the world and I was sorry to see us split after all those great years. I wanted our marriage to go on, but I had another woman in my life and that woman was my sons-in-law mom Vicki. She was great for me at the time understood me and we got along well. Vicki at the time we met was divorced and dating. She needed a place to live while she was buying our house on Midlane.

I talked to Robin, and she agreed that Vicki could live with us temporarily. Robin and I at that time were married for 18 great years 1982-2000 when I met Vicki. Vicki and I eventually started dating as my marriage to Robin became doomed for failure. In my opinion looking back and speaking for myself our marriage failed because of our interests outside our marriage started pulling us apart. Vicki and I were a better match. Vicki and I started to spend more time together eventually falling in love. Robin and I sold the house to Vicki for $80,000 and then later bought it back for $80,000 because she wanted to move to an apartment. We sold the house later for $100,000. In 2012 I moved in with Vicki at her apartment and we lived together until her death of brain cancer in 2017 at the age of 69.

The year was 2015 that Vicki and I took our first cruise together to the Bahamas aboard a Carnival Cruise Ship. It was great fun, and we really enjoyed the trip.

Photo by James Bruce

On the beach

On the ship Vicki shopping in the Bahamas

Photos by James Bruce

Photos by James Bruce

Vicki and Jim resting after a long walk. It was a beautiful week together and we had an exciting time. 2016 Vicki and I took another cruise to the Bahamas which included a trip to Mexico's Yucatan Peninsula.

Photos by James Bruce

Photos by James Bruce

While on our 2nd trip we visited a typical family in their home. We were told and shown their heating source being a pit in the ground. This house had no electric and for a bed they used hammocks. They prepared their own food which was organic and all natural. The family we visited prepared a natural Mexican dinner for us on the tour. The food was delicious, and we were very thankful for all the hospitality we received. We spent a day at the Mayan ruins, took a swim in a local pond located in the forest and paddled down a river to experience the wildlife and vegetation of the area. It was an exciting, planned, and interesting trip from start to finish. Truly a learning experience for both Vicki and me.

2014 WE CELEBRATED OUR first Great Grandchild in the birth of Gage Parker here with Grandma Chasity.

Photo by James Bruce

2017 We celebrated our second Great Grandchild in the birth of Hayley Parker. Pictured here with Great Great Grandmother Nan with Gage, Grandson Jacob and Granddaughter Courtney's mother of Gage and Hayley.

Photo by James Bruce

2017 started out another wonderful year doing what I love must and that was working at the Dispatch, managing a great new talent in Kalysta and spending time with Vicki. Next Vicki and I scheduled a trip to Vegas.

Las   Vegas,   Nevada

Photos by James Bruce

Shortly after our return, Vicki started having problems remembering what she was supposed to do at Walmart where she worked part-time. I came home one day and found Vicki at home trying to talk on the phone to one of her friends. I could tell by the conversation that she was having a hard time expressing herself and remembering who she was talking to. It was then that she told me that her manager at Walmart sent her home because she forgot what to do. I told her I thought we should make trip to Riverside Hospital to have things checked out. The doctors and nurses could tell things were not right. They told us that she needed was an x-ray of the brain to see if anything could be causing her problems. The results were scary, they found a large tumor that literally covered her entire upper brain plus 4 more on the lower half. Vicki's condition was considered terminal.

In the month of June, I went to visit Vicki at the nursing home where she was staying at because of brain cancer, a stroke and now diabetes has affected her body at the age of 69. But this was a special visit because she was happy, awake and eating some sherbet she obviously was enjoying and asked me "what was this stuff"? It made me laugh and she chuckled too. I had come into the room unexpected but with a smile enjoying her presence as I have for over 17 years. Some visits were uneventful, she slept a lot; we would hold hands at times and occasionally talk to each other mostly me doing the talking. She says things at times that do not make sense but that does not matter. It is her smile or a little laugh that matters now. I think she still recognizes me at times as she did this time. I said Hi, she said "What are you doing here"? Now she had me confused, but I carried on as if she does not. I noticed she was eating what looked like sherbet and really enjoying it much more than me being there. But that is ok, I still love her. I start this little conversation about how she felt, and she said OK. I told her about the visit I had with her yesterday and if she remembered me being there and she said, "a little bit". As I was enjoying our little visit and she, her sherbet, I told her how much I missed her, loved, and wished everything was as it was before they found that tumor in her brain. Vicki was enjoying her sherbet. Some days were better than others. I got up reached over and gave her a gentle kiss on the lips and she smiled as if that was a pleasant surprise not knowing if she knew who I was. I told her that I loved her and would be seeing her tomorrow. She told me "I'm sleepy." Vicki passed away Saturday July 22.

The Book & Music Publishing Business

James Paul Music Publishing (BMI) was established in 1994 to provide a copyright service for songwriters and generate royalty revenue for both the songwriters and the publishing company. I established James Paul Music, a publishing company through Broadcast Music Inc. (BMI) Nashville, Tennessee. James Paul Music was concerned with administering copyrights, licensing songs to record companies and others, and collecting royalties on behalf of the songwriter. Other services include issuing Mechanical, Synchronization and Print Licenses plus Song Plugging. I would like to thank Will Curtis for helping me for a couple of years before I terminated this company to concentrate on special projects in 2019.

I started James Paul Publishing (Books) in 2015. The worldwide book group has publishing connections worldwide. James Paul Publishing publishes new books in hard copy, paperback and digitally. Although James Paul Publishing concentrates on Children's fictional books, Adult fictional and non-fictional ebooks. My primary focus has been helping authors with self-publishing.

Today James Paul Publishing's authors and their work are at the center of everything I do. I am proud to provide our authors with unprecedented editorial excellence, marketing reach, connections with booksellers, and industry-leading insight into reader and consumer behavior. Consistently at the forefront of innovation and technological advancement, James Paul Publishing also uses digital technology to create unique reading experiences and expand the reach of our authors.

It has been my pleasure working with authors Pam Egbert and Christopher Eagan in promoting their books. Included are the books that I have promoted.

Author Pam Egbert and her books which I help promote.

Photos by ProDuctions/Pam Egbert

2   more   books   from   author   Pam   Egbert

Photos by ProDuctions/Pam Egbert

Author Christopher Eagan and his book I helped promote through social media and videos. Christopher is the husband of Diane Renay who recorded the #6 song in the USA back in 1963 call Navy Blue.

Photos by Christopher Eagan **Author Christopher Eagan**

Photo by Diane Renay

Navy Blue" is a song written by Bob Crewe[1], Bud Rehak and Eddie Rambeau[2]. The song tells the story of a girl who was lonely for her steady boyfriend while he was away from home in the U.S. Navy[3] and could hardly wait to see him again. The song's story is continued in "Kiss Me Sailor[4]."

Recorded in 1963 by pop singer Diane Renay[5] at the age of seventeen and released as a single, "Navy Blue" reached number six on the *Billboard* Hot 100[6] and topped the Middle-Road[7] singles chart for one week in March 1964.[1]8

1. https://en.wikipedia.org/wiki/Bob_Crewe

2. https://en.wikipedia.org/wiki/Eddie_Rambeau

3. https://en.wikipedia.org/wiki/United_States_Navy

4. https://en.wikipedia.org/wiki/Kiss_Me_Sailor

5. https://en.wikipedia.org/wiki/Diane_Renay

6. https://en.wikipedia.org/wiki/Billboard_Hot_100

7. https://en.wikipedia.org/wiki/Adult_Contemporary_(chart)

8. https://en.wikipedia.org/wiki/Navy_Blue_(Diane_Renay_song)#cite_note-AC-1

In Closing

More tragedy found my family in 2018 when my brother Ron died from heart complications. The following year 2019 I discovered that a girlfriend Helen Strah from the 70's had also passed at the age of 66 and my youngest brother Randy died from cancer in 2019 at the age of 67. That left Cliff (71) and I (74), Dianne (70), Linda (69), and Brenda (66).

Diane Jim Linda Cliff Brenda Cliff

Photos by James Bruce

In the year 2017, I met a girl at the Columbus Dispatch that was handling my old route and she asked me if I could sub her route. I said, "sure anytime she needed me, and I was available". Her name was Jennifer, and she was from West Virginia now living in Ohio with her brother. Jennifer and I had become good friends quickly and enjoyed our time together. We started going out to lunch and at times dinner then it progressed to going to the movie theatre. I invited and she accepted a trip to Las Vegas and another trip to Myrtle Beach, South Carolina both in 2018 and 2019. We had an exciting time on all trips. Our relationship as friends helped me get over the loss of Vicki, my family, and friends. Love was mentioned as our relationship grew but there was one problem, she was 42 and I was 74. I suggested she was my fantasy, and I was her reality and I let her decide where this relationship would take us. I think it became most complicated for both of us and she eventually decided we should separate for a while in February 2020. Keeping in touch, we have scheduled another trip in March 2023 to Key West, Florida. God Bless Everyone – No Exceptions.

I have had a wonderful life and I thank God for it just about every day.

Jennifer White Photos by James Bruce

Don't miss out!

Visit the website below and you can sign up to receive emails whenever James Bruce publishes a new book. There's no charge and no obligation.

https://books2read.com/r/B-A-XWUP-UWBRB

BOOKS 2 READ

Connecting independent readers to independent writers.

About the Author

About the Author by Marcia Ferko

Meet James Bruce, author, producer, agent, manager, business owner, and proud dad, grandpa, and great-grandpa. This accomplished individual's life story invites you to also seek and find the best of yours.

His generous, Christian and passionate heart for others has opened doors of opportunity and success for many. Through his own trial and error of failures and successes, he has shared his riches of wisdom with others. He has become an ambassador and liaison in both the private and professional settings and has been a mentor to many.

Through years of life experiences, Jim has become a conduit of knowledge for the past and the present. He tries to capture both as you read through his wealth of information here with him. We all can learn from each other's life and Jim's life is certainly a unique example of that.

His adventure is not through yet. His mantra still is "Dance while music is still playing and live your best life while it still lies before you!!!

Read more at https://jamespaulpublishin7.wixsite.com/jamespaul.